POWER STARS TO LIGHT THE FLAME

THE VISIONARIES AND YOU

THE BIG BOOK OF BUSINESS IDEAS, LEADERSHIP AND STRATEGIES

HOW TOP COMPANIES SUCCEED AND SUSTAIN

Hank Moore, Corporate Strategist

Power Stars to Light The Flame: The Visionaries and You is published
under Erudition Books, a sectionalized division under
Di Angelo Publications, Inc.

ERUDITION BOOKS

Erudition Books is an imprint of Di Angelo Publications.
Copyright 2012. Second Edition
All rights reservec.
Digital and print distribution in the United States of America.

Di Angelo Publications
4265 San Felipe #1100
Houston, Texas, 77027
www.diangelopublications.com

Library of Congress
Power Stars to Light the Flame: The Visionaries and You.
Paperback

ISBN: 978-1-942549-02-4

Interior Layout: Kimberly James
Words: Hank Moore

1. Business & Economics --- Leadership
2. Business & Economics --- Mentoring & Coaching
3. Business & Economics --- Motivational

United States of America with int. Distribution.

POWER STARS
TO LIGHT THE FLAME

THE VISIONARIES AND YOU

THE BIG BOOK OF BUSINESS IDEAS,

LEADERSHIP AND STRATEGIES

HOW TOP COMPANIES SUCCEED
AND SUSTAIN

Hank Moore, Corporate Strategist

TESTIMONIALS

"How can one person with so much insight into history and nostalgia be such a visionary? Hank Moore is one of the few who understands the connection."
- Dick Clark, broadcasting legend

"Hank Moore speaks from the brain and from the heart. I've personally observed his futuristic projections and insights since 1958."
- Lady Bird Johnson, former First Lady

"He is the only speaker or business advisor whom I heard this year who is truly the CEOs' peer. Hank Moore is the only one with an Ethics Statement, which CEOs understand and appreciate."
- Peter Bijur, Chairman, Texaco

"Hank Moore is a million dollar idea person. He is one of the few business experts whose work directly impacts a company's book value."
- Herb Kelleher, Chairman, Southwest Airlines

"Hank Moore's Business Tree⊠ is the most original business model of the last 40 years."
- Peter Drucker (2002)

"Hank Moore works miracles in changing stuck mindsets. He empowers knowledge from without by enthusing executives to reach within."
- Dino Nicandros, Chairman, Conoco

"Mr. Moore is one of the true authority figures for business and organization life. He is the only one with an Ethics Statement, which CEOs understand and appreciate."
- Ben Love, Vice Chairman, Chase Bank

"Your words of wisdom have reminded our members of those bigger issues which we sometimes overlook in the day-to-day performance of work."
- Thomas Gentry, American Institute of Architects

"I wanted to thank you wholeheartedly for including me in your dedication of your Business Tree book. I was honored to be a part of your book. That was a wonderful surprise."
- Bill Richardson, Governor of New Mexico

"Thank you for your expertise and commanding body of experiences. I always feel like I can conquer the world after reading your books."
- Letha Russell, President, Allegiant Energy Group, LP

"30 minutes with Hank is like 30 months with almost any other brilliant business guru. He's exceptional, unlike any other, and with a testimonial list to prove it. As a speaker, he's utterly content rich, no fluff, no 'feely-touchy' nonsense, right to the point and unashamed to tell the truth. There is nobody better. Every CEO needs him."
- Michael Hick, Director, Global Business Initiatives

"Hank Moore is a creative innovator. We have worked together in many client assignments and he continues to amaze me with his resourceful knowledge and application of inventiveness. As a member of a project team, leader, and expert resource, Hank provides a big picture perspective that is rare in business. If you want to see what is next for your business and be light years ahead in your strategy, contact Hank Moore immediately. He will provide you with long standing results." Top qualities: Great Results, Expert, Creative.
- Jackie Broussard, President, Great Ideas Company

"Hank Moore is an Excellent speaker and an outstanding business mentor. I cannot recommend him highly enough to those who are looking to get the very best out of the future by positioning themselves now. Hank as a wealth of experience."
- Mark Miller, Owner, Strategies For Success, Inc.

"I could not have wished for a better boss and mentor in my first professional job than Hank Moore. He leads by example, and taught me valuable lessons not only about business, but also professionalism and ethics that have stood me well throughout my career. Indeed, when I was in a position to mentor others, I've often repeated "Hank Moore stories" to my staff...they've all heard of my first boss. Over time, I grew to understand more and more that Hank Moore treats others with respect, and thereby commands respect. I was privileged to be trained by this creative and brilliant thinker who gets more accomplished in a day than most do in a week."

- *Heather Covault,* Media Relations Manager, Writer, Web Editor at Kolo, Koloist.com

CONTENTS

Introduction

Chapter 1   **17**

Adversity, Enemies, Competitors
Advice, Counsel
Age, Longevity, Wisdom
Ambition, Desire
Appearance, Image

Chapter 2   **35**

Beliefs, Convictions, Core Values
Blaming Others for One's Faults and Foilbles
Body of Knowledge, The Big Picture
Business

Chapter 3   **49**

Change, Proress
Choices
Courage
Courtesy, Customer Service, Corporate Manners
Creativity, Art

Chapter 4   **69**

Decisions
Details
Diversity
Education, Professional Development and
  Training
Ethics

Chapter 5   **85**

Facts
Failure
Fame, Branding, Corporate Image

Fear
Futurism, The Future

Chapter 6   **111**

Genius
Greatness, Quality
Heroes, Mentors, Role Models
History
Honesty
Hope
Human Nature

Chapter 7   **148**

Ideas
Knowledge
Language, Semantics, Labels
Laziness
Leadership
Lies

Chapter 8   **173**

Management
Mediocrity
Memory
Mistakes
Negotations, Compromise
Opportunity

Chapter 9   **197**

Perspectives on Life...Perceptions and Realities
Philanthropy, Charity, Community Involvement
Philosophy
Planning
Power
Pride

Chapter 10   **213**

Reputation
Respect

Responsibility and Accountability
Results, Benchmarking, Measurements
Rigidity—Reluctance to Progress

Chapter 11   **239**

Self Esteem, Confidence and Reliance
Simplicity
Statistics
Strength
Stress, Worry, Pain
Substance, Depth
Success
Survival

Chapter 12   **261**

Tact
Talent, Potential
Teamwork, Collaborations, Partnering
Technology
Temptation
Thinking
Time
Trust, Relationship Building
Truth, Understanding

Chapter 13   **289**

Values, Ideals
Vision
Work
Youth

Closing Quotes   **307**

About the Author   **311**

INTRODUCTION

Business is at a most decisive crossroads. Corporate scandals and mistrust in business puts all of us in the position of picking up the pieces and moving forward.

The rules have changed—always have and always will. A great many mosaics make up The Big Picture. Yet the wider perspective in business is rarely seen. Too many myopic niches dominate the view.

This book is about widening the scope much further. Whenever we review what made the business successful, we see that Big Picture thinking took part in past times, before the micro mindsets took over.

The potentiality of organizations is a progressive journey from information to insight. Foolhardiness is being all righteous about inconsequential things at the wrong times. People and organizations spend disproportionate amounts of time trying to behave like or look like someone else...or what they think others appear to be. Until one becomes one's own best role model, the futile trail will continue.

When you and your company widen the scope and advocate strategic planning and visioning, I will have fulfilled my mentoring role. Futuristic ideas can and should become your ideas, mindset and ethical business practice.

This is a compendium book, containing quotes and extrapolations into business culture from history's biggest names, including Thomas Jefferson, William Shakespeare, Yogi Berra, Albert Einstein, John F. Kennedy, Bob Dylan, Thomas Payne, Franklin Roosevelt, John Steinbeck, Proverbs, Winston Churchill, Henry Kissinger, etc. Quotes are broad- based, for maximum appeal.

This book offers the quotes for motivation. It also functions as a

"PDR of business," a wide-scope view of Big Picture strategies, methodologies and recommendations. It also contains sage advice that the leadership quote books do not encompass.
By doing a compendium of big names, then we do something novel for the leadership book market. It has pop culture appeal. It also includes a full array of business strategies not found in niche-oriented books. This is intended as a textbook for the mass business market.

This book covers leadership, business psychology, team-building, quality management, empowerment, community stewardship and marketplace development. Recurring themes for business survival, strategies, growth and vision will be intertwined with the quotes and anecdotes.

Quotes and analysis are applicable to stages in the evolution of a business, leadership development and mentoring. This is a creative way of re-treading old knowledge to enable executives to master change, rather than feel as they're victims of it.

Business in the 21st Century is real and dangerous. People suddenly feel lost and not in a safe port. They don't know how to cope. Yesterday's strategies don't work anymore.

Many of the old assumptions have proven untrue and unworkable. We really must examine what we assumed before and what we can assume now. Business is at a juncture and needs wider focus. This book views the whole of the organization, then the parts and back to the sum.

It's a whole new world. Pressures continue and accelerate for companies to stay in operation, become competitive, keep ahead of the marketplace and perform quality work. Businesses of all sizes are besieged with opportunities, competing information sources and large amounts of uncertainty. Executives are not really prepared to handle challenges of the moment...much less to begin developing Big Picture thinking.

We must re-examine how to keep score in the New Order of

Business. Most of the downfalls, trips, false starts and incorrect handling of situations are attributable to business' lack of focus on the macro...and too much emphasis upon certain micros, to the exclusion of other dynamics.

This book states the case for a Big Picture-focused approach to business management. A thorough re-examination of the corporate culture encompasses much more than accounting fraud and stated values of stocks.

The time is now for fresh thinking, heightened ethical behavior and a shift to a macro focus. Rules and responsibilities within each sector of companies are changing. Each of us must ask what we can contribute and our roles in adapting to the business crises. What we do with fear and uncertainty determines what our organizations become in the future.

CHAPTER 1

Adversity, Enemies, Competitors
Advice, Council
Age, Longevity, Wisdom
Ambition, Desires
Appearances, Image

ADVERSITY, ENEMIES, COMPETITORS

"A man cannot be too careful in the choice of his enemies."
- *Oscar Wilde*

"Under conditions of tyranny, it is easier to act than to think."
- *Hannah Arendt*

"All men would be tyrants if they could."
- *Daniel Defoe*

"Truth forever on the scaffold. Wrong forever on the throne."
- *James Russell Lowell*

"Any excuse will serve a tyrant."
- *Aesop*

"Better a thousand enemies outside the house than one inside."
- *Arabic proverb*

"Even a paranoid can have enemies."
- *Henry Kissinger*

"He makes a friend who never had a foe."
- *Alfred Lord Tennyson*

"If you have no enemies, then fortune has not smiled upon you."
- *William Shakespeare*

Adversity, Enemies, Competitors

Every business and community in America is presently at a crossroads. Recent business events should generally be seen as a beacon for planning, reflection and optimistic venturing toward the future.

There exist two current options for businesses:

1. Each organization can be seen and known as a dynamic community that addresses its problems and moves forward in a heroic fashion...as a role model to the rest of the world.

Or,

2. Organizations can bury their heads in the sand and hope media attention dies down...thus becoming a generic tagline for troubled business waters.

Undoubtedly, most of us want to choose option one and seek complex answers for the judicious practices of moving forward.

Volatile business contractions, uneasy economic climate, plant explosions, health care crises, hostile corporate takeovers, governmental shakeups, and financial failings are crises that upset the routine of business life. These occurrences or their variations are feared by the business community. Some jolting incident puts every organization into a reaction mode. The consequences of miscommunication in a crisis can be devastating to all involved.

By dealing with the unexpected, preferably before it occurs, companies can bank public goodwill that may be useful later. Playing catch-up means that you have lost the game.

Among the types of crises that I have advised clients include government reorganizations, plant explosions, contaminated food and drugs, school shootings, executive kidnappings, installation bombings, hostile company takeovers, natural disasters and problematic employee behaviors. In doing so, I have learned that strategic planning for crises can avert the worst 85% of the time. In times of crisis, business does what it should have done earlier: study, reflect, plan and manage change.

It is the responsibility of corporate management to practice effective Crisis Management and Preparedness. Management must study practical experiences of what can go wrong, put a crisis team into place, understand the workings of news media, identify community opinion leaders, and predict potentially harmful or controversial situations.

Comprehension of the dangers includes case studies of how other corporations handled emergencies. Learn from those who were successful, those who failed to achieve the desired effects, and those whose corporate credibilities were damaged by doing nothing.

We learn a lot from our competitors, including those whom we respect and those in whom we do not put much stock. They are our competitors for many reasons. The ideal planning process looks squarely at the marketplaces and analyzes why all players succeed and fail. These nuggets of wisdom serve as basis for our own future successes.

ADVICE, COUNSEL

"No one wants advice...only collaboration."

- John Steinbeck

"A good scare is worth more than good advice. He that has no children brings them up well."

- Proverbs

"Advice is seldom welcome. Those who want it the most always like it the best."

- Earl of Chesterfield

"Most people get advice. Only the few smart ones profit from it."
- Daniel Webster

"Do not criticize your government when out of the country. Never cease to do so when at home."
- Sir Winston Churchill

"Your business is to put me out of business."
- President Dwight D. Eisenhower

"I intended to give you some advice but now I remember how much is left over from last year unused."
- George Harris

"One gives nothing so freely as advice."
- Duc de la Rochefoucauld

"It's queer how ready people always are with advice in any real or imaginary emergency. No matter how many times experience has shown them to be wrong, they continue to set forth their opinions, as if they had received them from the Almighty."
- Annie Sullivan

"There is nothing we receive with so much reluctance as advice."
- Joseph Addison

"When we ask advice, we are usually looking for an accomplice."
- Marquis de Lagrange

"People ask you for criticism, but they only want praise."
- W. Somerset Maugham

Advice, Counsel

Selecting the most appropriate consultant for your company— optimizing expertise—is the greatest challenge facing a decision maker.

It's lonely at the top. Certain kinds of objective information cannot come from within your own camp. True expertise is a rare commodity, and the successful company utilizes it on the front end, rather than on the costly back end. There are the seven plateaus of advice given to business leaders. with #1 being the base level of advice and #7 being the most insightful:

1. Answers to Questions. There are 7 levels of answers which may be given, depending upon how extensive one wants: Easy and Obvious Ones, Knee-Jerk Reactions, Politically Correct, What People Want to Hear, Factual and Complete Explanations, Answers That Get Them Thinking Further and Deep Wisdom.

2. Observations on Situations. These take the forms of "When this happened to me, I did X," or "If this occurred with me, I would Y." It's often good to see things through someone else's perspective.

3. Subjective Viewpoint. Friends want what is best for you. This level of advice is usually pro-active and is influenced by the advisor's experiences with comparable situations.

4. Informed Opinion. Experts have core-business backgrounds upon which to draw. Advisors bring facts, analysis and methodologies of applying their solutions to your case. Niche consultants provide quality viewpoints...as it relates to their talents and skills. Carefully consider the sources.

5. Researched Options. Investments in research (formal, informal, attitudinal, demographic, sociological) will avert unnecessary band-aid surgery expenses later. Research leads to planning, which is the best way to accomplish tasks and benchmark success.

6. Discussion of Outcomes—Consequences. Most actions and decisions in an organization affect many others. At this level, advisors recommend that sufficient planning be conducted... please take their advice. The more strategic and Big Picture in scope, then planning reaps long-term rewards.

7. Inspiring Directions. This gets into Visioning. Planning and going to new heights are stimulating. The mannerisms and substance by which any organization achieves its Vision requires sophisticated advice, deep insights and creative ideas.

Matching consultants with actual and emerging company needs is the corporate leader's quest. With a wealth of expertise available via outsourcing, one can quickly become a "kid in a candy shop," wanting whatever is readily available or craftily packaged.

Too many consultants   mis-state and   o v e r - r e p r e s e n t what they do, stemming from:
  - Eagerness to get business.
  - Short tenure in consulting, believing that recent corporate experience readily translates to the tentrepreneurial marketplace.
  - Unfamiliarity with the actual practice of consulting at the executive level.
  - Lack of understanding about business needs, categories, subtleties and hierachies.
  - Failure to create service area niches and target clients.
  - Professional rivalry with other consultants, resulting in the "I can do that" syndrome.

Everyone knows that dentists, nurses, social workers and respiratory therapists are all health care professionals. Yet, distinctions in their expertise lead consumers to discern and seek out specialists...or at least ask a general practitioner physician to make referrals for necessary services.

Niche consultants place emphasis in the areas where they have training, expertise and staff support for implementation... and will market their services accordingly. An accounting firm may suggest that an economic forecast is a full-scope business plan (which it is not). A trainer may recommend courses for human behavior, believing that these constitute a Visioning process (of which they are a small part). Marketers might contend that the latest advertising campaign is equivalent to re-engineering the client company (though the two concepts are light years apart).

Niche consultants believe these things to be true, within their frames of reference. They sell what they need to sell, rather than what the client really needs. Let the buyer beware.

— AGE, LONGEVITY, WISDOM —

"Life begins at 40."
> *- Sophie Tucker*

"Never too late to learn. There's many a good tune played on an old fiddle."
> *- Proverbs*

"An adult is one who has ceased to grow vertically but not horizontally. You've reached middle age when all you exercise is caution."
> *- Proverbs*

"The only thing I regret about my past life is the length of it. If I had my past life over again, I'd make all the same mistakes... only sooner."
> *- Tallulah Bankhead*

"Man arrives as a novice at each age of his life."
> *- Nicolas Chamfort*

"Middle age is youth without its levity and age without decay."
> *- Writer Daniel Defoe*

"Youth is a blunder, manhood a struggle, old age a regret."
> *- Benjamin Disreali, statesman*

"Middle age is when your age starts to show around the middle."

- Bob Hope

"At 20 years of age, the will reigns; at 30, the wit; and at 40, the judgment."

- Benjamin Franklin

"The four stages of man are infancy, childhood, adolescence and obsolescence."

- Art Linkletter

"All that the young can do for the old is to shock them and keep them up to date."

- George Bernard Shaw

Age, Longevity, Wisdom

Everything we are in business stems from what we've been taught or not taught to date. A career is all about devoting resources to amplifying talents and abilities, with relevancy toward a viable end result.

Amassing a Body of Knowledge—which leads to Wisdom —is a long and enjoyable process. It is the first step toward a career-life Strategy, which evolves into a Vision. Using a corporate analogy, a Mission Statement is 1% of a Strategic Plan, which is 20% of a Visioning Program.

Business evolution is an amalgamation of thoughts, technologies, approaches and commitment of the people, asking such tough questions as:

1. What would you like for you and your organization to become?

2. How important is it to build an organization well, rather than

constantly spend time in managing conflict?

3. Who are the customers?

4. Do successful corporations operate without a strategy-vision?

5. Do you and your organization presently have a strategy-vision?

6. Are businesses really looking for creative ideas? Why?

7. If no change occurs, is the research and self-reflection worth anything?

Most of us learned about business (which is a compendium of life relationships) "in the streets." Today's business leaders entered and pursued careers without a strategic plan or service manual. Professionals pursue many approaches to garnering information and, ultimately, to unlocking the answers that inevitably lie within. Methods include seminars, books, consultations, professional association involvement, training, organizational development, executive roundtables, civic activities and much more.

Failure to prepare for the future spells certain death for businesses and industries in which they function. The same analogies apply to personal lives, careers and Body of Work. Greater business awareness and heightened self awareness are compatible and part of a holistic journey of growth.

None of us can escape those pervasive influences that have affected our lives. Like sponges, we absorbed information and perceptions of life that have helped mold our business and personal relationships.

AMBITION, DESIRE

"Ambition should be made of sterner stuff."
- William Shakespeare

"I would sooner fail than not be among the greatest."
- John Keats

"He who rides a tiger is afraid to dismount."
- Proverb

"There is always room at the top."
- Daniel Webster

"A man's reach should exceed his grasp. Man partly is and wholly hopes to be."
- Robert Browning

"If you would hit the mark, you must aim a little above it. Every arrow that flies feels the attraction of earth. Most people would succeed in small things if they were not troubled with great ambitions."
- Henry Wadsworth Longfellow

"Ambition is a poor excuse for not having sense enough to be lazy."
- Edgar Bergen

"Women who seek to be equal with men lack ambition."
- Timothy Leary

"Hitch your wagon to a star. Without ambition one starts nothing. Without work one finishes nothing. The prize will not be sent to you. You have to win it. The man who knows how will always have a job. The man who also knows why will always be his boss. As to methods, there may be a million and then some, but principles are few. The man who grasps principles

can successfully select his own methods. The man who tries methods, ignoring principles, is sure to have trouble."
- Ralph Waldo Emerson

"Ambition often puts men upon doing the meanest offices; so climbing is performed in the same posture with creeping."
- Jonathan Swift

"Keep away from people who try to belittle your ambitions. Small people always do that, but the really great make you feel that you, too, can become great."
- Mark Twain

"A man without ambition is dead. A man with ambition but no love is dead. A man with ambition and love for his blessings here on earth is ever so alive. Having been alive, it won't be so hard in the end to lie down and rest."
- Pearl Bailey

"Live neither in the past nor in the future, but let each day's work absorb your entire energies, and satisfy your widest ambition."
- Sir William Osler

"Ambition drove many men to become false; to have one thought locked in the breast, another ready on the tongue."
- Sallust, "The War with Catiline"

"He who, blinded by ambition, raises himself to a position whence he cannot mount higher, must thereafter fall with the greatest loss."
- Niccolo Machiavelli

"All ambitions are lawful except those which climb upward on the miseries or credulities of mankind."
- William Congreve

"You despise books; you whose lives are absorbed in the vanities of ambition, the pursuit of pleasure or indolence; but remember that all the known world, excepting only savage nations, is governed by books."

- Voltaire

"Though ambition itself be a vice, yet it is often times the cause of virtues."

- Quintilian

"Character cannot be developed in ease and quiet. Only through experience of trial and suffering can the soul be strengthened, ambition inspired, and success achieved."

- Helen Keller

Ambition, Desire

Fine-tuning one's career is an admirable and necessary process. It is not torture but, indeed, is quite illuminating. Imagine going back to reflect upon all you were taught.

Along the way, you reapply old knowledge, find some new nuggets and create your own philosophies.
We were taught to be our best and have strong ambition to succeed. Unfortunately, we were not taught the best methods of working with others in achieving desired goals. We became a society of highly ambitious achievers without the full roster of resources to facilitate steady success.

Lacking ambitions or misplaced ambitions account for the great business tragedies that profoundly affect the economy and blemish the marketplace.

══ **APPEARANCES, IMAGE** ══

"All that glitters is not gold. Men should be what they seem. Through tattered clothes, small vices do appear. Robes and furred gowns hide all."

- William Shakespeare

"Handsome is as handsome does. Fine feathers make fine birds. A man need not look in your mouth to know how old you are. Never judge from appearances. You can't tell a book by its cover. Vice is often clothed in virtue's habit. Appearances are deceptive."

- Proverbs

"At 50, everyone has the face he deserves."

- George Orwell

"Things are entirely what they appear to be, and behind them, there is nothing."

- Jean-Paul Sartre

"The world is governed more by appearances than realities, so that it is fully as necessary to seem to know something as to know it."

- Daniel Webster

"Beware so long as you live, of judging people by appearances."
- La Fontaine

"Do not judge men by mere appearances; for the light laughter that bubbles on the lip often mantles over the depths of sadness, and the serious look may be the sober veil that covers a divine peace and joy."

- E. H. Chapin

"Appearances often are deceiving."
- Aesop, "The Wolf in Sheep's Clothing"

"Fashion is the science of appearances, and it inspires one with the desire to seem rather than to be."

- Michel de Montaigne

"Do not hover always on the surface of things, nor take up

suddenly, with mere appearances; but penetrate into the depth of matters, as far as your time and circumstances allow, especially in those things which relate to your profession."

- Isaac Watts

"It is only shallow people who do not judge by appearances."

- Oscar Wilde

"By listening to his language of his locality the poet begins to learn his craft. It is his function to lift, by use of imagination and the language he hears, the material conditions and appearances of his environment to the sphere of the intelligence where they will have new currency."

- William Carlos Williams

Appearances, Image

Every organization must and should put its best foot forward for the public.

These are the seven plateaus that most leaders reach in addressing their image and public opinions of their organizations:

1. Those Resulting from Doing Nothing. The biggest problem with business, in a one-sentence capsule, is: People exhibit misplaced priorities and impatience, seeking profit and power, possessing unrealistic views of life, and not fully willing to do the things necessary to sustain orderly growth and long-term success.

2. Doing Things As We Always Have. This leads to stifled Visioning attempts, stagnant company image, obsolete policies-procedures, procrastination about taking pro-active positions, in-actions, resistance to innovation and failure to change.

3. Selling, Marketing, Promoting.

4. Spin Doctoring. Organizations and individuals try to put "spins" on situations in order to meet crises and benefit their immediate interests. Such situations are complicated through: (a) Refusal to take action, (b) Letting problems fester until they become diseases, (c) Lack of accountability, (d) Waiting until it is too late to avert a crisis, (e) Taking correctional measures after too much damage has been done, (f) Waiting too late to make good for damage.

5. Taking an Educational Stance. Informing the marketplace about their industry, business and products. Consumers with more informed opinions will be in a better position to do business with your company.

6. Being an Informed, Enlightened Citizen. Being successful in business for the long haul goes beyond just communicating what the organization does. A well planned and executed public affairs program sculpts how the organization will progress, its character and spirit, participation of its people and steps that will carry the organization to the next tiers of desired achievement, involvement and quality.

7. Raising the Standards, Going the Distance. Communications practices begin with forethought, continues with research and culminates in a plan, incorporating and enriching the mission, core values, goals and objectives of the organization.

As companies adjust comfort levels and acquire confidence in the arena of business development, there is a direct relationship of the success of corporate communications to billings, client mix diversity, market share, competitive advantage, stock price and levels of business which enable other planned growth.

Public perceptions are called "credence goods" by economists. Every organization must educate outside publics about what they do and how they do it. This premise also holds true for each corporate operating unit and department. The whole of the business and each sub-set must always educate corporate opinion makers on how it functions and the skill with which the company operates.

Gaining confidence among stakeholders is crucial. Business relationships with customers, collaborators and other professionals are established to be long-term in duration. Each organization or should determine and craft its own corporate culture, character and personality, seeking to differentiate itself from others.

Top management must endorse corporate communications if your company is to grow and prosper. Few companies can even sustain present levels of sales without some degree of business development.

CHAPTER 2

Beliefs, Convictions, Core Values
Blaming Others for One's Faults and Foibles
Body of Knowledge, The Big Picture
Business

BELIEFS, CONVICTIONS, CORE VALUES

"The will to do, the soul to dare."

- Sir Walter Scott

"Stand. In the end, you'll still be you. One that's done all the things you set out to do. There's a cross for you to bear⬚ things to go through, if you're going anywhere. There's a giant inside of you, about to grow. Stand. Don't you know you are free. Well, at least in your mind, if you want to be."

- Sly & the Family Stone

"Be always sure you're right...and then go ahead."

- Davy Crockett

"Men are alike in their promises. It is only in their deeds that they differ."

- Moliere

"One must learn by doing the thing. Though you think you know it, you have no certainty until you try."

- Sophocles

"I had rather be right than President."

- Henry Clay

"No act of kindness, no matter how small, is ever wasted. Kindness affects more than severity."

- Aesop

"If you will it, it is no dream."

- Theodor Herzl

"Our wills and fates do so contrary run that our devices still are overthrown. Our thoughts are ours, their ends none of our own."

- William Shakespeare

Beliefs, Convictions, Core Values

How organizations start out and what they become are different concepts. Mistakes, niche orientation and lack of planning lead businesses to failure. Processes, trends, fads, perceived stresses and "the system" force managers to make compromises in order to proceed. Often, a fresh look at previous knowledge gives renewed insight.

The purpose of re-examining and refining Core Values is to:
- Think Big Picture.
- Conceptualize and communicate your company's own goals.
- Understand conflicting societal goals.
- Fit your dreams into the necessities and realities of the real world.
- Find your own niche...do your thing.
- Get satisfaction from doing something well and committing to long-term excellence.
- Seek truths in unusual and unexpected sources.
- Share your knowledge, and learn further by virtue of mentoring others.

In many industries and professions, business development has occurred primarily by accident or through market demand. Because of economic realities and the increased numbers of firms providing comparable services, the notion of business development is now a necessity, rather than a luxury. Competition for customers/clients is sharpening. The professions are no longer held on a pedestal, a condition which mandates them to portray or enhance their core values.

I would encourage business leaders to fill out a Core Values Worksheet These are the key criteria for basing your professional vision:

1. Core Industry...The Business You're In.
2. Rendering the Service...Administering Your Work.
3. Accountability...Qualities with Which You Work.

37

4. Your Relationships-Contributions to Other People...
    Colleagues, Stakeholders.
5. Professional-Leadership Development...Your   Path to
    the Future.
6. Your Contributions to the Organization's Overall
    Goals...Your Place in its Big Picture.
7. Body of Work.. Your Accomplishments to Date
    and Anticipated Future Output.

BLAMING OTHERS FOR ONE'S
══ FAULTS AND FOIBLES ══

"Everybody wants to blame it on someone else. So they say,
'The devil made me do it.' He is too busy being smothered by
people who are surrounding him and asking him what to do
to have the time to go someplace and find somebody and tell
them to do something."

- Flip Wilson

"Only a person with a criminal enterprise deserves to establish
an alibi."

- Sherlock Holmes

Blaming Others for One's
Faults and Foibles

Some people and organizations go to great extremes to place
spins, rationalize or save face in their business lives. Often,
sweeping generalizations involve making far-fetched excuses
or scapegoating someone else.

Criticizing others may be cloaked as a subtle or even polite
dialog. Yet, behind these often-voiced expressions lie fallacies

in reasoning, the wrong facts, jealousy, animosity, personal self-defeat or cluelessness of the speaker.

When people pose scapegoatish statements, they generally are made to cover up their own failure to make investments in future company success. They might rationalize organizational setbacks, poor service or quality imperfections. Those who blame problems upon others may be avoiding change and denying the need for change. If such proclaimers were engaged in planning for future operations, they would not be blamers.

During two years of corporate scandals, some have blamed business schools for turning out graduates programmed to increase shareholder value at any price. But if a key to business success is the ability to adapt to changing circumstances, then business schools are now demonstrating that quality. Many are now integrating ethics into existing programs and training courses. I applaud that trend and ask that more be taught about corporate citizenship and the critical executive mastery skills. Also, retain more adjuncts with real-world business savvy. Having myself functioned periodically as an adjunct since 1971, I value the mentoring opportunities with fresh minds who will be future leaders in the New Order of Business.

It's not about who caused the problems. It is all about who is doing something to stop them. Those who resist taking proactive measures and persist in playing the Blame Game are the sabotagers of corporate success. By refocusing upon the opportunities, rather than being stuck in bureaucratic paralysis, the company can make strides.

These are the ways to avoid negatively voiced euphemisms:
- Put more emphasis upon substance, rather than flash and sizzle.
- Look outside the organization, instead of keeping your total focus internal.
- Challenge negative comments and make the accusers accountable for their own organizational

progress.
- Keep communications open and continual.
- Refrain from making false representations.
- The abilities to think, reason, take risks and feel gut instincts must all be nurtured.
- Take advise from all sources. Do your research. Get informed counsel from seasoned advisors inside and outside of your industry.
- Document and comprehend reasons for successes.
- Cite case studies often.
- Empower the organization to embrace-embody the corporate culture.
- Learn to manage change, rather than become a victim of it.

BODY OF KNOWLEDGE, THE BIG PICTURE

"The cosmic process has no sort of relation to moral ends."
- T.H. Huxley

"O amazement of things...even the least particle!"
- Walt Whitman

"Virtue, study and gaiety are three sisters who should not be separated."
- Voltaire

"My will was to live worthily as long as I lived, and after my life to leave them that should come after, my memory in good works."
- Boethius

"It is a far, far better thing that I do, than I have ever done. It is a far, far better rest that I go to, than I have ever known."
- Charles Dickens

"Wisdom comes only through suffering. Wonder is the beginning of wisdom."

- Greek proverbs

"The fox knows many things, but the hedgehog knows one great thing."

- Archilochus

"Knowledge comes, but wisdom lingers."
- Alfred, Lord Tennyson

"Nine-tenths of wisdom consists in being wise in time."
- President Theodore Roosevelt

"Be wiser than other people if you can, but do not tell them so."
- Earl of Chesterfield

"The world is full of people who are not wise enough."
- La Fontaine

"It is a characteristic of wisdom not to do desperate things."
- Henry David Thoreau

"The highest wisdom has but one science...the science of the whole...the science explaining the whole creation and man's place in it."

- Leo Tolstoy

"The bitter and the sweet come from the outside, the hard from within, from one's own efforts."

- Albert Einstein

"Learning is a treasure which accompanies its owner everywhere."

- Chinese proverb

Body of Knowledge, The Big Picture

It seems so basic and so simple: Look at the whole of the organization, then at the parts as components of the whole and back to the bigger picture.

I advocate planning ahead and taking the widest possible view... very common-sense and utilizing a series of bite-sized chunks of business growth activity. This is the approach to clients that I have taken as a senior business advisor for 40 years. Even in times of crisis or when working on small projects, I use every opportunity to inspire clients look at their Big Pictures. The typical reaction is that my approach makes sense, and why haven't others taken it before.

The Big Picture can and does exist, though companies have not found it for their own applications very often. Organizations know that such a context is out there, but most search in vein for partial answers to a puzzling mosaic of business activity. The result, most often, is that organizations spin their wheels on inactivity, without crystallizing the right balance that might inspire success.

Obsession with certain pieces, comfort levels with other pieces and lack of artistic flair (business savvy) keep the work in progress but not resulting in a finished masterpiece.

Businesses rarely start the day with every intention of focusing upon the Big Picture. They don't get that far. It is too easy to get bogged down with minutia. This book and my advising activities are predicated upon educating the pitfalls of narrow focus and enlightening organizations on the rewards of widening the view.

Should every business become Big Picture focused? Yes. My job is to widen the frame of reference as much as possible. Under a health care model, I am the internist, a diagnostician who knows about the parts and makes informed judgments about the whole. This enables the specialists to then be more successful in their treatments, knowing that they stem from an accurate diagnosis and prescription.

Alas, the Big Picture of business is a continuing realignment of current conditions, diced with opportunities. The result will be creative new variations. Masterpieces are not stagnant paintings...they can be continually evolving works in progress.

═══════ BUSINESS ═══════

"No nation was ever ruined by trade."

- Benjamin Franklin

"Trade is a social act."

- John Stuart Mill

"The business of America is business."
- President Calvin Coolidge

"There is no such thing as a free lunch."

- Milton Friedman

"If you pay peanuts, you get monkeys."

- James Goldsmith

"The big print giveth, and the fine print taketh away."
- Bishop J. Fulton Sheen

"If two men on the same job agree all the time, then one is useless. If they disagree all the time, them both are useless."
- Darryl F. Zanuck

"Business underlies everything in our national life, including our spiritual life. Witness the fact that in the Lord's Prayer, the first petition is for daily bread. No one can worship God or love his neighbor on an empty stomach."
- President Woodrow Wilson

"The first mistake in public business is the going into it."
- Benjamin Franklin

"Disbelief in magic can force a poor soul into believing in government and business."
- Tom Robbins

"The harder the conflict, the more glorious the triumph. What we obtain too cheap, we esteem too lightly; it is dearness only that gives everything its value. I love the man that can smile in trouble, that can gather strength from distress and grow brave by reflection. 'Tis the business of little minds to shrink; but he whose heart is firm, and whose conscience approves his conduct, will pursue his principles unto death."
- Thomas Paine

"If you want to succeed, you'd better look as if you mean business."
- Jeanne Holm

"No one can possibly achieve any real and lasting success or "get rich" in business by being a conformist."
- J. Paul Getty

"If I had to sum up in one word what makes a good manager, I'd say decisiveness. You can use the fanciest computers to gather the numbers, but in the end you have to set a timetable and act."
- Robert P. Vanderpoel

"The most successful businessman is the man who holds onto the old just as long as it is good, and grabs the new just as soon as it is better."
- Lee Iacocca

"Any business arrangement that is not profitable to the other person will in the end prove unprofitable for you. The bargain that yields mutual satisfaction is the only one that is apt to be repeated."
- B. C. Forbes

"The successful man is the one who finds out what is the matter with his business before his competitors do."
- Roy L. Smith

"A friendship founded on business is better than a business founded on friendship."
- John D. Rockefeller, Jr.

"The person who knows how will always have a job. The person who knows why will always be his boss."
- Diane Ravitch

"Politics is the art of preventing people from sticking their noses in things that are properly their business."
- Paul Valéry

"For a long time it had seemed to me that life was about to begin—real life. But there was always some obstacle in the way. Something to be got through first, some unfinished business, time still to be served, a debt to be paid. Then life would begin. At last it dawned on me that these obstacles were my life."
- Alfred D'Souza

"Our business in life is not to get ahead of others, but to get ahead of ourselves—to break our own records, to outstrip our yesterday by our today."
- Stewart B. Johnson

Business

There is a difference between knowing a product-industry and growing a successful business. It is possible for a company and its managers to know much about certain arts and sciences without having the will to pursue them.

Organizations do not set out to go bad. They just don't "set out" (little or no planning). Thus, they go off course. These are the major areas where companies fail, per branch on The Business Tree™:

1. The business you're in. They are not in the right business for well-thought-out reasons. They don't have a clearly unique product, but instead rally behind ideas that are not fully developed. There exists either an overdependence upon one product or service line, or the company is diversifying beyond the scope of its core expertise.

2. Running the business. One observes poor controls, obsolete equipment and under-qualified administrative support. Staff is not properly trained or equipped to handle rapid influxes of business. Production and deliverability are strained already... and it gets worse.

3. Financial. The company is undercapitalized. It may experience unprofitable pricing, poor payables-receivables policies, lack of accountability and excess overhead. There is too much emphasis upon getting rich, rather than steadily growing and improving. Management relies only upon "bean counters" for company direction.

4. People. There exists a misuse of company resources, notably its people. Insufficient investment was made toward human capital on the front end. Employees are not empowered to make decisions or take risks. Management remains isolated or unrealistic, possessing limited leadership development and people skills.

5. Business Development. There exists an overall naivete about the marketplace, reflected by unrealistic sales policies, quotas and sales management. Customer service is not good, doesn't improve and never is a major emphasis for the company. Marketing is more for ego reasons, rather than a careful strategy. Sales and marketing are not given enough support...especially management's personal participation. There is a lack of understanding about protecting existing business, entering new markets, new product development or

collaborations.

6. Body of Knowledge. The organization has fought change. It is unable to read the warning signs or understand external influences. Regulatory red tape proliferates. Management doesn't take the time to understand how the company has grown or analyze the relationship of each branch to the other. The company has set itself up to avoid change...failing to grow without a crafted or shared Vision.

7. The Big Picture. The company has failed to understand what business they're really in. They have not planned strategically. Without an articulated, well-implemented vision, business will not evolve because no Big Picture ever existed.

Much of the wisdom to succeed lies within. It must be recognized, fine-tuned and utilized. Much of the wisdom to succeed lies outside your company. It must be called upon, sooner rather than later.

People under-perform because they are not given sufficient direction, nurturing, standards of accountability, recognition and encouragement to out-distance themselves. Organizations start to crumble when their people quit on each other.

Unhealthy organizations will always "shoot the messenger" when change and improvements are introduced. Healthy organizations absorb all the knowledge and insight they can, embracing change, continuous quality improvement and planned growth.
Anybody can poke holes in an organization. The art-skill is to create programs and systems which do something constructive.

The level of achievement by a company is commensurate to the level and quality of its vision, goals and tactics. The higher its integrity and character, the higher its people must aspire.

CHAPTER 3

Change, Progress
Choices
Courage
Courtesy, Customer Service, Corporate Manners
Creativity, Art

CHANGE, PROGRESS

"Nature's mighty law is change."

- Robert Burns

"Nothing's the same when you see it again."
- Cat Stevens, "Portobello Road"

"Change is inevitable in a progressive society. Change is constant."

- Benjamin Disraeli

"Change is not made without inconvenience, even from worse to better."

- Richard Hooker

"You can't step twice into the same river. Everything flows, and nothing stays still."

- Heraclitus

"The basic fact of today is the tremendous pace of change in human life."

- Jawaharlal Nehru

"He that will not apply new remedies must expect new evils. For time is the greatest innovator."

- Sir Francis Bacon

"All progress is precarious, and the solution of one problem brings us face to face with another problem."
- Martin Luther King, Jr.

"Human progress is furthered, not by conformity, but by aberration."

- H.L. Mencken

"Chaos often breeds life, when order breeds habit."
                                    - Henry Brooks Adams

Change, Progress

Research shows that change is 90% positive and that individuals and organizations change at the rate of 71% per year.

Change is necessitated by a natural flow of events, stemming from changes already made and realized. Some changes are mandated by others in control, and others are necessitated by circumstances outside your control.

The worst blockages of change come from people who possess the "been there, done that" attitude. Eighty-seven percent of the time, they really haven't. Other spoilers include middle managers who can't see the forest for the trees, don't want to see beyond the scope and are proud of it.

Young generations who grow up in the houses of the above group see and emulate the anti-change constituencies. They grow up not knowing any better, clinging to the status quos and acting out their limited scope in the classrooms, in social settings and in their early business careers (until they learn better).

Young people in the business world (up to age 40) tend to want instant results, instant gratification and the success of people their senior who have paid substantial dues. As they learn to benefit from change, they mellow into savvy business executives.

To those who block processes of organizational change, things will pass you by, with or without your efforts. Negative efforts will harm your potential for success. Mastering change sooner rather than later has beneficial effects, with no down side.

companies and careers. It accelerates the learning curve and success ratio. Those who do not get on the bandwagon will not last in the company. Those who excel develop leadership skills, empowered teams and efficiencies.

Leaders who expose their teams to new territories helps them see how they adapt within that framework. Championing change can mark the next tier in an executive's development.

A well-intentioned person may want and try so hard to do the right thing that he-she makes mistakes and ultimately does the wrong thing. It is the mark of a great person to admit mistakes, correct the course and move on. Another mark of a great leader is to let his people lead too...and give them the reins to do so effectively.

Change helps you do business in the present and helps plan for the future. Without mastering he challenges of a changing world, companies will not be optimally successful.

The company/organization which manages change remains successful, ahead of the competition and is a business/industry leader. Meanwhile, other companies will have become victims of change because they stood by and did nothing.

CHOICES

"The United States will always make the right choice...but only after choosing other options first."
- Sir Winston Churchill

"If you limit your choices only to what seems possible or reasonable, you disconnect yourself from what you truly want, and all that is left is a compromise."
- Robert Fritz

"Because you are in control of your life, don't ever forget

that you are what you are because of the conscious and subconscious choices you have made."
- *Barbara Hall,* "A Summons to New Orleans"

"It is our choices that show what we truly are, far more than our abilities."
- *J. K. Rowling*, "Harry Potter and The Chamber of Secrets"

"Honor isn't about making the right choices. It's about dealing with the consequences."
- *Midori Koto*

"In all things, there are three choices: Yes, No & no choice, except in this, I either choose the truth or I am deceit."
- *Sovereign*

"The future is not a result of choices among alternative paths offered by the present, but a place that is created--created first in the mind and will, created next in activity. The future is not some place we are going to, but one we are creating. The paths are not to be found, but made, and the activity of making them, changes both the maker and the destination."
- *John Schaar*

"If we could raise one generation with unconditional love, there would be no Hitlers. We need to teach the next generation of children from Day One that they are responsible for their lives. Mankind's greatest gift, also its greatest curse, is that we have free choice. We can make our choices built from love or from fear."
- *Dr. Elizabeth Kubler-Ross*

"Most people receive very little training on how to live effectively and harmoniously with themselves and others. This I believe is an unfortunate outcome of our parenting beliefs and methods, as well as society's educational systems. It seems to me these beliefs and systems empathize academic and vocational skills and place little or no emphasis or value on providing a person with the essential skills to live a life of personal fulfillment, contribution and self actualization. I believe it would be a safe assumption that the great majority of people work at jobs in which they find very little personal satisfaction.

Without proper training on how to make wise choices in one's life, the chances are very slim anyone will make them."

- Sidney Madwed

"Every person has free choice. Free to obey or disobey the Natural Laws. Your choice determines the consequences. Nobody ever did, or ever will, escape the consequences of his choices."

- Alfred A. Montapert

Choices

These are the seven levels of choices that we can make:
1. Past choices made..how you've evolved.
2. Good choices...and why they worked.
3. Bad choices...lessons learned.
4. Against your will.
5. For the good of the project, career, company.
6. For your own good.
7. Taking charge...responsible choices.

COURAGE

"Courage is resistance to fear, mastery of fear--not absence of fear."

- Mark Twain

"Courage is the price that life exacts for granting peace."

- Amelia Earhart

"We could never learn to be brave and patient. If there were

only joy in the world."
- Helen Keller

"In the dark days and darker nights when England stood alone, and most men save Englishmen despaired of England's life, he mobilized the English language and sent it into battle."
- President John F. Kennedy

"I was not the lion. But it fell to me to give the lion his roar."
- Sir Winston Churchill

"Courage and perseverance have a magical talisman, before which difficulties disappear and obstacles vanish into air."
- President John Quincy Adams

"Courage is the ladder on which all the other virtues mount."
- Clare Booth Luce

"Life shrinks or expands in proportion to one's courage."
- Anais Nin

"I wanted you to see what real courage is, instead of getting the idea that courage is a man with a gun in his hand. It's when you know you're licked before you begin but you begin anyway and you see it through no matter what."
- Harper Lee, "To Kill a Mockingbird"

"Every human being on this earth is born with a tragedy, and it isn't original sin. He's born with the tragedy that he has to grow up. That he has to leave the nest, the security, and go out to do battle. He has to lose everything that is lovely and fight for a new loveliness of his own making, and it's a tragedy. A lot of people don't have the courage to do it."
- Helen Hayes

"Discouragement is simply the despair of wounded self- love."
- Francois de Fenelon

"Difficulties are meant to rouse, not discourage. The human

spirit is to grow strong by conflict."

- William Ellery Channing

"The bravest thing you can do when you are not brave is to profess courage and act accordingly."

- Corra Harris

"When you meet your antagonist, do everything in a mild and agreeable manner. Let your courage be as keen, but at the same time as polished, as your sword."

- Richard Brinsley Sheridan

"If you explore beneath shyness or party chit-chat, you can sometimes turn a dull exchange into an intriguing one. I've found this to be particularly true in the case of professors or intellectuals, who are full of fascinating information, but need encouragement before they'll divulge it."

- Joyce Carol Oates

"Have courage for the great sorrows of life and patience for the small ones; and when you have laboriously accomplished your daily task, go to sleep in peace."

- Victor Hugo

"Never discourage anyone who continually makes progress, no matter how slow."

- Plato

"You gain strength, courage and confidence by every experience in which you really stop to look fear in the face. You say to yourself, I have lived through this horror. I can take the next thing that comes along. You must do the thing you think you cannot do."

- Eleanor Roosevelt

"Keep your fears to yourself, but share your courage with others."

- Robert Louis Stevenson

"Discourage litigation. Persuade your neighbors to compromise whenever you can. As a peacemaker the lawyer has superior opportunity of being a good man. There will still be business enough."

- President Abraham Lincoln

"Have patience with all things, but chiefly have patience with yourself. Do not lose courage in considering you own imperfections but instantly set about remedying them. Every day begin the task anew."

- Saint Francis de Sales

"Courage is doing what you're afraid to do. There can be no courage unless you're scared."

- Eddie Rickenbacker

"It is curious that physical courage should be so common in the world and moral courage so rare."

- Mark Twain

"Courage is being scared to death...but saddling up anyway."

- John Wayne

"Please write again soon. Though my own life is filled with activity, letters encourage momentary escape into others lives and I come back to my own with greater contentment."

- Elizabeth Forsythe Hailey, "A Woman of Independent Means"

Courage

These are the stages in people's courage to learn and commit to new perspectives on life and business:

1. Cluelessness, Apathy. Henry Ford said, "90% of the American people are satisfied." Will Rogers said, "Mr. Ford is wrong. 90% of the people don't give a damn." Content with the status quo. Taking a vacation from thinking. Not

interested in learning more about life or seeing beyond one's realm of familiarization.

2. Basic Awareness. Latent readiness. Not moved to think differently, take risks or make decisions until circumstances force it. 90% don't care about specific issues until events that affect their lives force them to care about something. 5% affect decisions. 5% provide momentum.

3. Might Consider. The more one gathers information, they apply the outcomes of selected issues to their own circumstances. Begin learning through message repetitions.

4. Taking in Information. Something becomes familiar after hearing it seven times. Gains importance to the individual through accelerated familiarity. The more one learns, the more one realizes what they don't know. At this plateau, they either slide back into the denial level of cluelessness or launch a quest to become mature via learning more about life.

5. Courage to Form Opinions. Triggering events or life changes cause one to consider new ideas, ways of thinking. Survival and the need-desire for self-fulfillment causes one to form strong desires to learn. Cluelessness and inertia are no longer options and are now seen as backward and self- defeating.

6. Thinking and Analyzing. Changing paradigms. Behavioral modification ensues. There are ways we used to think and behave. We do these things differently now because we have learned preferable ways that cause better outcomes. Thus, we don't revert to the old paradigms.

7. Behavioral Change and Commitment. Advocating positions. Creating own original ideas. Holding and further developing insights. Commitment to change and personal growth. Willing and able to teach and share intellect and wisdom with others.

COURTESY, CUSTOMER SERVICE, CORPORATE MANNERS

"The customer is always right."

- H. Gordon Selfridge

"The greater man, the greater courtesy."

- Alfred Lord Tennyson

"There are two little words that can open any door with ease.One little word is thanks, and the other is please. Good manners are never out of style."

- Pinky Lee

"We are born charming, fresh and spontaneous and must be civilized before we are fit to participate in society. It is far more impressive when others discover your good qualities without your help. Let us make a special effort to stop communicating with each other, so we can have some conversation."

- Judith Martin (Miss Manners)

"We don't bother much about dress and manners in England, because as a nation we don't dress well and we've no manners."

- George Bernard Shaw

"Good manners will open doors that the best education cannot."

- Supreme Court Justice Clarence Thomas

"Do thou restrain the haughty spirit in thy breast, for better far is gentle courtesy."

- Homer

"Don't forget to say please and thank you."

- Captain Kangaroo

"Don't flatter yourself that friendship authorizes you to say disagreeable things to your intimates. The nearer you come into relation with a person, the more necessary do tact and courtesy become. Except in cases of necessity, which are rare, leave your friend to learn unpleasant things from his enemies; they are ready enough to tell them."
- Supreme Court Justice Oliver Wendell Holmes

"Gratitude is the most exquisite form of courtesy."
- Jacques Maritain

"All legislation, all government, all society is founded upon the principle of mutual concession, politeness, comity, courtesy; upon these everything is based. Let him who elevates himself above humanity, above its weaknesses, its infirmities, its wants, its necessities, say, if he pleases, I will never compromise; but let no one who is not above the frailties of our common nature disdain compromises."
- Henry Clay

"Discourtesy does not spring merely from one bad quality, but from several--from foolish vanity, from ignorance of what is due to others, from indolence, from stupidity, from distraction of thought, from contempt of others, from jealousy."
- Jean de la Bruyere

"Don't reserve your best behavior for special occasions. You can't have two sets of manners, two social codes—one for those you admire and want to impress, another for those whom you consider unimportant. You must be the same to all people."
- Lillian Eichler Watson

"Associate with well-mannered persons and your manners will improve. Run around with decent folk and your own decent instincts will be strengthened."
- Stanley Walker

"Manners maketh man."
> *- Motto of Winchester College and New College, Oxford*

"History is a voice forever sounding across the centuries the laws of right and wrong. Opinions alter, manners change, creeds rise and fall, but the moral law is written on the tablets of eternity."
> *- James A. Forude*

Courtesy, Customer Service, Corporate Manners

In today's highly competitive business environment, every dynamic of a successful organization must be toward ultimate customers. Customer focused management goes beyond service and quality. There is no business that cannot improve its customer orientation. Every organization has customers, clients, stakeholders, financiers, volunteers, supporters or other categories of "affected constituencies."

Customer focused management is a concept that goes far beyond just smiling, answering queries and communicating with buyers. It transcends customer service training. In today's highly competitive business environment, every dynamic of a successful organization must be toward ultimate customers.

Companies must change their focus from products and processes toward the values which they share with customers. Customer focused management goes beyond just the dynamics of service and quality.

Everyone with whom you conduct business is a customer or referral source of someone else. The service that we get from some people, we pass along to others. Customer service is a continuum of human behaviors shared with those whom we meet.

Customers are the lifeblood of every business. Employees depend upon customers for their paychecks. Yet, you wouldn't know the correlation when poor customer service is rendered. Employees of companies behave as though customers are a bother, do not heed their concerns and do not take suggestions for improvement.

There is no business that cannot undergo some improvement in its customer orientation. Every organization has customers, clients, stakeholders, financiers, volunteers, supporters or other categories of "affected constituency."

CREATIVITY, ART

"Creativity is a drug I cannot live without."
- *Cecil B. DeMille*

"The secret to creativity is knowing how to hide your sources."
- *Albert Einstein*

"Frugality without creativity is deprivation."
- *Amy Dacyczyn*

"Creativity can solve almost any problem. The creative act, the defeat of habit by originality, overcomes everything."
- *George Lois*

"Creativity represents a miraculous coming together of the uninhibited energy of the child with it apparent opposite and enemy, the sense of order imposed on the disciplined adult intelligence."
- *Norman Podhoretz*

"Creativity is allowing yourself to make mistakes. Art is knowing which ones to keep."
- *Scott Adams*, "The Dilbert Principle"

"Above all, we are coming to understand that the arts incarnate the creativity of a free people. When the creative impulse cannot flourish, when it cannot freely select its methods and objects, when it is deprived of spontaneity, then society severs the root of art. In free society, art is not a weapon. Artists are not engineers of the soul. This nation cannot afford to be materially rich and spiritually poor."

- President John F. Kennedy

"When Alexander the Great visited Diogenes and asked whether he could do anything for the famed teacher, Diogenes replied: 'Only stand out of my light.' Perhaps some day we shall know how to heighten creativity. Until then, one of the best things we can do for creative men and women is to stand out of their light."

- John W. Gardner

"Creativity is...seeing something that doesn't exist already. You need to find out how you can bring it into being and that way be a playmate with God."

- Michele Shea

"Creativity comes from trust. Trust your instincts."

- Rita Mae Brown

"While we have the gift of life, it seems to me that only tragedy is to allow part of us to die, whether it is our spirit, our creativity, or our glorious uniqueness."

- Comedienne Gilda Radner

"Curiosity is the key to creativity."

- Akio Morita, "Made in Japan"

"My curiosity is my creativity on the way to discovery. A hunch is creativity trying to tell you something."

- Proverbs

"Creativity is the power to connect the seemingly unconnected."

- William Plomer

Hank Moore

"Don't think. Thinking is the enemy of creativity. It's self-conscious, and anything self-conscious is lousy. You can't try to do things. You simply must do things."

- Ray Bradbury

"You must not for one instant give up the effort to build new lives for yourselves. Creativity means to push open the heavy, groaning doorway to life. This is not an easy struggle. Indeed, it may be the most difficult task in the world, for opening the door to your own life is, in the end, more difficult than opening the doors to the mysteries of the universe."

- Daisaku Ikeda

"When we are angry or depressed in our creativity, we have misplaced our power. We have allowed someone else to determine our worth, and then we are angry at being undervalued."

- Julia Cameron, "The Vein of Gold"

"Nothing can be created out of nothing."

- Lucretius

"Wisdom comes by disillusionment."

- George Santayana, "Reason in Common Sense"

"Brevity is the soul of wit."

- William Shakespeare

"The object of art is to give life shape."

- Jean Anouilh

"The lower one's vitality, the more sensitive one is to great art."

- Max Beerbohlm

"Art for art's sake."

- Victor Cousin

"Art is a microscope which the artist fixes on the secrets of his soul and shows to people these secrets which are common to all."

- Leo Tolstoy

"That willing syspension of disbelief for the moment, which constitutes poetic faith."

- Samuel Taylor Coleridge

"Art is a jealous mistress."

- Ralph Waldo Emerson

"No artist is ahead of his time. He is his time. It is just that others are behind the times."

- Martha Graham

"The pain passes, but the beauty remains."

- Pierre Auguste Renoir

Creativity, Art

Along with knowledge of the industry in which one works, there is a creative art to being effective at every aspect of running and sustaining each facet of a successful business. These are details per each of the seven categories on my trademarked Business Tree™:

Branch 1: The business you're in. There are skills attached to rendering the service or manufacturing the products. People get into businesses because they have expertise in an area, such as widget making. It is for this that they have received education, training, professional development, mentoring and much more. Business founders and leaders are good at making widgets and are exceedingly comfortable with Branch 1.

The art comes in amassing professional abilities, specialties and skills in working with industry consultants, technical specialists, sub-contractors, vendors and core business suppliers.

Branch 2: Running the business. This involves administrative practices, procedures, operations, structure, the physical plant, technologies, equipment, supplies and distribution. Once people get onto Branch 2, the problems begin and start to multiply. Few widget experts are taught how to manufacture widgets and deliver them to market. Nor, are widget makers really taught the multi-dynamics of actually operating a business. Hence, all decisions are made from a Branch 1 perspective, mentality and orientation.

The art comes in working with lawyers, engineers, technology experts, non-core business suppliers, communications providers and repair-maintenance companies.

Branch 3: Financial Components include cash flow forecasting, budgeting, equity and debt financing, accounting, record keeping, banking and investing.

No company stays in business without money...incoming and, to a hopefully lesser degree, outgoing. Making money is not the only reason for being in business. Usually, it's to make the best possible widgets and, then, to be very successful at it. Financial expertise helps Branch 1 founders stay focused upon fiduciary responsibilities.

Branch 4: People. Leadership tasks include recruiting, hiring and supervision. Companies are successful by possessing an attained art to human resources management, empowerment, team building, training, incentives and professional executive development.

This is the largest and most under-nourished branch on the tree. Organizations cannot operate with people. However, many organizations tend to misuse, ignore, ill-advise, misguide, neglect and mistreat the people working for and with them. Employees are most often hired for Branch 1 expertise and put to work. Like the company founders, most widget experts are not well versed in the other branches of the tree. Even in their Branch 4 interface with other employees, they function from a

Branch 1 vantage.

There is an art to motivating people and optimizing their performance. Research studies show that money is rarely the primary motivation for people in careers and their professional lives. All people in the organization need lots of professional attention, mentoring, training and administrative support. Few ever get their needs satisfied, and thus, companies realize reduced work output and a less-than-zealous attitude.

Management cries, "Fix those people," without realizing that they are a large part of the problem. All of us can stand having our people skills refined. That's why widget makers, administrative staff, bean counters and all other leaves on the tree must embrace empowerment, team building, open communication and other concepts to relate better to human beings.

Branch 5: Business development. The components include corporate imaging, marketplace perceptions and realities, sales, marketing, public relations, advertising and research.

One cannot stay in business unless they market and sell something. Branch 1 creators think incorrectly that they are in the "widget" business. Actually, they are in the "widget manufacturing and marketing" business. Many companies are principally in the "widget marketing" business. Having a better widget is but a small part of that equation.

Branch 1 experts in management tend to fight marketing and sales, branding those two different professional specialties as necessary evils that someone else must deal with. The astute upper management will integrate all five branches and participates personally in Branch 5...taking their widget to market.

Using another analogy, a person who gives birth and does nothing more toward their child is not a good parent. That person is successful after shepherding the offspring through the various stages of growth and facets of life.

Categories 6 and 7 are the nurturing-strength (basis of business), which enable Branches 1, 2, 3, 4 and 5 to interrelate and function most successfully.

Category 6 (trunk): Body of Knowledge. The components include professional development, product-service development, external influences and information, collaborations, partnering, joint venturing, government, regulating factors, marketplace limitors, community standards and niche constituencies.

No company can stay in business without understanding the relationship of each branch (business function) to the other, each limb (department) to the other, each twig (niche consultant) to the other, each leaf (employee) to the other and each part of the Business Tree has its proper responsibility and should learn to interface with the others.

This sophisticated and vital category includes research and consultation with management on external forces affecting company growth, mostly outside their control but which can limit business opportunities. There is an art to fine-tuning the processes by which management gains new insight about the future of business, viabilities for change management, emerging issues and the next necessary steps. This category also includes crisis management and preparedness programs and the building of strategic business alliances.

Category 7 (roots): The Big Picture. The components include building a shared vision, corporate responsibility, creative business practices, strategic planning, innovations, outside-the-box thinking, the quality process, ethics, changing markets and walking the talk.

The successful company takes the time and appropriates the resources to develop a Big Picture. This costs one-sixth that of continually applying "band aid surgery" to problems as they arise. Business is approached as a Body of Work...a lifetime track record of accomplishments.

CHAPTER 4

Decisions
Details
Diversity
Education, Professional Development and Training
Ethics

DECISIONS

"The die is cast."

- Julius Caesar

"If someone tells you he is going to make 'a realistic decision,' you immediately understand that he has resolved to do something bad."

- Mary McCarthy

"In a minute, there is time for decisions and revisions, which a minute can reverse."

- T.S. Eliot

"No trumpets sound when the important decisions of our life are made. Destiny is made known silently."

- Agnes DeMille

"Good plans shape good decisions. That's why good planning helps to make elusive dreams come true."

- Lester R. Bittel, "The Nine Master Keys of Management"

"Trust: Just as you would not want to do business with someone you can't trust, this law simply stated is: When you can completely trust the process of the universe and life, you will be supplied abundantly and you will be able to make your life work just the way you want it. And the trust you give and have must be 100% or it is zero. It cannot be given under one condition and not under another. There are many things we trust with our lives and have no concern about.

Such as: the sun will come up every day; the law of gravity works all the time; the pilot who pilots the plane we fly on, is competent; our garbage is picked up on certain days. If we could not trust the things we take for granted will occur without any effort on our part, the fear for our well being would be so great we would not be able to enjoy our lives.

Can you imagine what the world would be like, if we could

not trust the food we buy, the water we drink or that the people we depend on would not manipulate or harm us? But the only way we can expect others to trust us is, we need to be trustworthy ourselves, and especially to ourselves.

Unfortunately, many people don't trust themselves and the judgments and decisions they make. Therefore, they experience disharmony with their lives and their world."

- Sidney Madwed

"It is a poor wit who lives by borrowing the words, decisions, inventions and actions of others."

- Johann Kaspar Lavater

Decisions

Most of our energies are spent on reacting to the latest crisis, putting out fires and placing focus upon the most minute pieces of the puzzle. That's why human beings and companies spend six times more on "band-aid surgery" each year than if they planned ahead on the front end. That's why one-third of our Gross National Product is spent each year on cleaning up mistakes.

In business, I explain to senior management in Big Picture perspectives the concepts behind the activities which the employees and consultants are conducting. For diversity, team building, sales, quality, customer service, training, technology, marketing and all the rest to be optimally successful, they must fit within a context, a plan and a corporate culture.

Will every business become Big Picture focused? No, because vested interests and human nature want to keep attention on the small pieces. Those organizations with the wider horizons and the most creative mosaic of the small pieces will stand out as the biggest successes.

The Big Picture provides leadership for progress, rather than following along. The successful organization develops and champions the tools to change. The quest is to manage change, rather than falling the victim of it. Such activities cannot be studied, visioned or developed in-house. Branch consultants cannot or should not be utilized at this level.

DETAILS

"Little things affect little minds."

- Benjamin Disraeli

"Little things are infinitely the most important."

- Sir Arthur Conan Doyle

"Our life is frittered away by detail. Simplify, simplify."

- Henry David Thoreau

"A little neglect may breed great mischief. For the want of a nail, a shoe was lost. For the want of a shoe, the horse was lost. For the want of a horse, the rider was lost."

- Benjamin Franklin

"Men who love wisdom should acquaint themselves with a great many particulars."

- Heraclitus

"Blow me a kiss from across the room. Say I look nice when I'm not. A line a day when you're far away. Little things mean a lot."

- Kitty Kallen

"One should absorb the color of life, but one should never remember its details. Details are always vulgar."

- Oscar Wilde, "The Picture of Dorian Gray"

"After all it is those who have a deep and real inner life who are best able to deal with the irritating details of outer life."

- Evelyn Underhill

"Beware of the man who won't be bothered with details."
- William Feather

"My religion consists of a humble admiration of the illimitable superior spirit who reveals himself in the slight details we are able to perceive with our frail and feeble mind. That deeply emotional conviction of the presence of a superior reasoning power, which is revealed in the incomprehensible universe, forms my idea of God. I want to know God's thoughts...the rest are details."
- Albert Einstein

"I am a design chauvinist. I believe that good design is magical and not to be lightly tinkered with. The difference between a great design and a lousy one is in the meshing of the thousand details that either fit or don't, and the spirit of the passionate intellect that has tied them together, or tried. That's why programming—or buying software—on the basis of "lists of features" is a doomed and misguided effort. The features can be thrown together, as in a garbage can, or carefully laid together and interwoven in elegant unification, as in APL, or the Forth language, or the game of chess."
- Ted Nelson

"Clever liars give details, but the cleverest don't."
- Author Unknown

"The great successful men have used their imaginations, they think ahead and create their mental picture, and then go to work materializing that picture in all its details, filling in here, adding a little there, altering this a bit and that bit, but steadily building, steadily building."
- Robert Collier

Details

One must look at the Big Picture of business first, then at the pieces as they relate to the whole.

There is a difference between knowing a product-industry and growing a successful business. It is possible for a company and its managers to know much about certain arts and sciences without having the will to pursue them.

Organizations do not set out to go bad. They just don't "set out" (little or no planning). Thus, they go off course. Much of the wisdom to succeed lies within. It must be recognized, fine-tuned and utilized. Much of the wisdom to succeed lies outside your company. It must be called upon, sooner rather than later.

People under-perform because they are not given sufficient direction, nurturing, standards of accountability, recognition and encouragement to out-distance themselves. Organizations start to crumble when their people quit on each other.

Unhealthy organizations will always "shoot the messenger" when change and improvements are introduced. Healthy organizations absorb all the knowledge and insight they can... embracing change, continuous quality improvement and planned growth.

The level of achievement by a company is commensurate to the level and quality of its vision, goals and tactics. The higher its integrity and character, the higher its people must aspire.

════ **DIVERSITY** ════

"What is food to one is to another bitter poison."

- Lucretius

"Variety's the very spice of life, that gives it all its flavor."

- William Cowper, The Task

"Letting a hundred flowers blossom and a hundred schools of thought contend is the policy."

- Mao Tse-tung

"No pleasure lasts long unless there is variety to it."

- Pubililius Syrus

"It were not best that we should all think alike. It is difference of opinion that makes horse races."

- Mark Twain

"Everyone is a prisoner of his own experiences. No one can eliminate prejudices - just recognize them."

- Edward R. Murrow

"Diversity is the one true thing we all have in common. Celebrate it every day."

- Anonymous

"When power leads man towards arrogance, poetry reminds him of his limitations. When power narrows the area of man's concern, poetry reminds him of the richness and diversity of his existence. When power corrupts, poetry cleanses."

- President John F. Kennedy

Diversity

Several years ago, we realized that specialized positioning and communications are necessary for social harmony and a global economy. We are a diverse population, and the same ways of communicating do not have desired effects anymore.

Diversity is about so much more than human resources issues. It means making the most of the organization that we can. It means being anything that we want to be. Diversity is NOT about quotas and should NEVER be perceived as imposed punishment. By taking stock and planning creatively, then we can and will embody diversity.

The premise of multicultural diversity is ambitious and necessary to achieve. It is a mindset that must permeate organizations from top-down as well as bottom-up. If not pursued in a sophisticated, sensitive way, good intentions will be wasted.

The following pointers are offered to companies who communicate with niche publics:

- Seek and train multi-cultural professionals.

- Contribute to education in minority schools...assuring that the pipeline of promising talent can rise to challenges of the workforce.

- Design public relations programs that embrace multicultural constituencies, rather than secondarily appeal to them after the fact.

- Interface with community based groups, sharing in activities and civic service...to learn how communications will be received.

- Realize that minority groups are highly diverse. Not every Asian knows each other, nor speaks the same language. There are as many subtle differences in every ethnic group as the next. Thus, multicultural communicating is highly customized.

- Realize that multi-cultural communications applies to all. Black professionals do not just participate in African American community events. Cultivate White and Hispanic communicators toward cross-culturization.

- As media does a good job of showcasing multicultural events, note it positively. If thanked enough, media will continue to shine the light on multicultural diversity.

- Sophistication in the gauging of public opinion will result in a higher caliber of communicating. The demands of an ever-changing world require that continuous improvement be made. Attention paid to writing and graphics quality will enhance the value of multicultural communications.

The old theory was that society is a Melting Pot. That philosophy evolved to the Salad Bowl concept. In either, one element still sinks to the bottom. We must now see it as a Mosaic or Patchwork Quilt. Each element blends and supports others. Diversity is a continuing process where we keep the elements mixed.

People believe that they are now thinking differently and creatively about diversity issues. In truth, they are really rearranging their existing prejudices. To be diverse and united, societies must be sealed with common purposes.
We can be diversified and unified at the same time. We can remain culturally diversified. We still can and should work together as a society. We all hold cultural values. One set is not better than another.

Look at the issues and how they affect the total person. Actions are always required. Good intentions and political correctness are not enough.

It is short sighted to ignore changes in society. It is good business to recognize opportunities for practice development. In the Chinese culture, every crisis is first recognized as a danger signal and always as an opportunity for overcoming obstacles.

Every professional must embrace a set of ethics:
- Things for which each professional holds himself/ herself accountable.
- Holds benchmarks for Continuous Quality Improvement.
- Realistically attainable goals.
- Contains mechanisms to teach and mentor others.

- Continually re-examines and adds to the list.

There are many good reasons why diversity relates to your livelihood:
- Embracing diversity is politically correct.
- Society will make increasing demands that you address these issues.
- It makes good business sense.
- It opens your services to additional market niches.
- It embodies the spirit of open communications, the basis of winning companies.
- This process creates more job opportunities for multicultural professionals.
- And it is the right thing to do.

=EDUCATION, PROFESSIONAL= DEVELOPMENT AND TRAINING

"Soon learned, soon forgotten."

- Proverb

"Knowledge itself is power. Studies serve for delight, ornament, and ability."

- Sir Francis Bacon

"Education is the best provision for old age."

- Aristotle

"They know enough who know how to learn. A teacher affects eternity and can never tell where his influence stops."

- Henry Brooks Adams

"The direction in which education starts a man will determine his future life."

- Plato

"Education is simply the soul of a society as it passes from one generation to another."

- G.K. Chesterton

"I have learned since to be a better student, and to be ready to say to my fellow students, 'I do not know.'"

- William Osler

"He who can does. He who cannot, teaches."

- George Bernard Shaw

"Training is everything. The peach was once a bitter almond. Cauliflower is nothing but a cabbage with a college education. Soap and education are not as sudden as a massacre, but they are more deadly in the long run."

- Mark Twain

"Human history becomes more and more a race between education and catastrophe."

- H.G. Wells

"Wisdom is ofttimes nearer when we stoop than when we soar."

- William Wordsworth

"What we have to learn to do, we learn by doing."

- Aristotle

"I am always ready to learn although I do not always like being taught."

- Sir Winston Churchill

Education, Professional Development and Training

Professional development is the most important ingredient in corporate progress. Today's workforce will need three times the amount of training that it now gets if the organization intends to stay in business, remain competitive and tackle the future successfully.

Each year, one-third of the Gross National Product goes toward cleaning up problems, damages and the high costs of doing either nothing or the wrong things. Half of that amount goes toward some form of persuasion, instruction, spin-doctoring or educating.

More often that not, "training" is a vehicle to tout one's viewpoint, tinker with old problems or blame someone else for the course of events. If training is viewed as band-aid surgery to fix problems, then it will fail. Managers who have this "fix those people" mindset are, in fact, the ones who need substantive training the most.

Professional development is rarely allowed to be extensive. It is usually technical or sales-marketing in nature. Employees and executives are rarely mentored on the people skills necessary to have a winning team. Thus, they fail to establish a company vision and miss their business mark.

Outside of "think tanks" for company executive committees, full-scope education does not occur. This is primarily because niche trainers recommend what they have to sell, rather than what the company needs. Niche trainers impart their own perspectives out of context to the whole of the organization.

There is a difference between how one is basically educated and the ingredients needed to succeed in the long-term. Many people never amass those ingredients because they stop learning or don't see the need to go any further. Many people think they are "going further" but otherwise spin their wheels. There is a large disconnect between indoctrinating people to tools of the trade and the myriad of elements they will need to assimilate for their own futures.

Neither teachers nor students have all the necessary ingredients. It is up to both to obtain skills, inspiration, mentoring, processes, accountability, creativity and other components from niche experts.

Therein lies the problem. Training vendors sell what they have to provide...not what the constituencies or workforces need. Emphasis must be placed upon properly diagnosing the organization as a whole and then prescribing treatments for the whole, as well as the parts.

ETHICS

"The end must justify the means."

- Matthew Prior

"If I am not what I say I am, then you are not what you think you are."

- novelist James Baldwin

"What is moral is what you feel good after. What is immoral is what you feel bad after."

- Ernest Hemingway

"Virtue is not always amiable. The happiness of man, as well as his dignity, consists in virtue."

- President John Adams

"Very often, our virtues are only vices in disguise."

- La Rochefougauld

"Always do right. This will gratify some people and astonish the rest."

- Mark Twain

"The laugh is always on the loser." German proverb "The function of wisdom is discriminating between good and evil."

- Cicero

Hank Moore

"Ethical axioms are found and tested not very differently from the axioms of science. Truth is what stands the test of experience."
- *Albert Einstein*

"The humblest citizen in all of the land, when clad in the armor of a righteous cause, is stronger than all the hosts of error."
- *William Jennings Bryan*

"We can act as if there were a God; feel as if we were free; consider nature as if she were full of special designs; lay plans as if we were to be immortal; and we find then that these words do make a genuine difference in our moral life."
- *William James*

"We must learn to distinguish morality from moralizing."
- *Henry Kissinger*

"Any preoccupation with ideas of what is right or wrong in conduct shows an arrested intellectual development."
- *Oscar Wilde*

Ethics

Ethics is the science of morals, rightness and obligations in human affairs. Institutions must conduct many activities which impact their general welfare. Ethical issues go beyond nice rhetorics and must encompass duties, principles, values, processes, responsibilities and governing methodologies.

Companies who fail to address ethical issues of the day are endangered species. Whatever the public expects of companies, then those companies should expect the same of themselves.

The company's Ethics Statement must be more than a terse branding slogan. Like the Mission Statement in the Strategic Plan, it is the amalgamation of careful thought, weighed insights and tests for fairness and durability. The Ethics Statement must be a part of the Strategic Plan, as are such other fundamental statements covering customer-focused management, diversity, valuing stakeholders, quality management and an empowered workforce.

Every organization differs in how it will implement Corporate Responsibility and Ethics programs. The differences are factored by the company's size, sector, culture and the commitment of its leadership. Some companies focus on a single area of operation. The Code of Ethics may include Fundamental Canons, Rules of Practice and Professional Obligations.

Business ethics encompass much more than accounting fraud and the publicly stated values of stocks. Ethics should be attached to many other important areas of business. Elements in the Ethics internal company review, which could subsequently be addressed in the full ethics plan, contained within the company's overall Strategic Plan.

The corporate ethics program may include a code of ethics, training for employees for ethical behaviors, a means for communicating with employees, reporting mechanism, audit system, investigation system, compliance strategy, prevention strategy and integrity strategy. The program seeks to create conditions that support the right actions. It communicates the values and vision of the organization. It aligns the standards of employees with those of the organization. The program relies upon the entire management team, not just the legal and compliance personnel.

A formal and well documented corporate ethics program will prevent ethical misconduct, monetary losses and losses to reputation. If communicated well, it may breed customer trust. In fact, I highly recommend using executive summaries of the ethics program as a corporate communications tool. Sending the Ethics Statement to customers, suppliers, regulators and other stakeholders demonstrates the extra length to which the company goes to become a model. It becomes a good marketing mailing, and it's the right thing to do.

As part of strategic planning, corporate ethics helps the organization to adapt to rapid change, regulatory changes, mergers and global competition. It helps to manage relations with stakeholders. It enlightens partners and suppliers about a company's own standards. It reassures other stakeholders as to the company's intent.

Managers must balance efficiency, effectiveness and change management. Efficiency means doing things right. Effectiveness means doing the right things. Change management seeks to empower people and optimize resources so that the organization will benefit from change, rather than become a victim of it.

Responsible companies should inspire executives to think holistically about each component of the business in terms of the Big Picture, master change and take companies to new tiers. Executives should inspire their companies to take fresh approaches toward re-applying past knowledge and experiences. As part of the planning process, they should develop strategies to reduce band-aid surgery approaches to problems...making business more creative, effective and profitable.

CHAPTER 5

Facts
Failure
Fame, Branding, Corporate Image
Fear
Futurism, The Future

FACTS

"Facts speak louder than statistics."

- Geoffrey Streatfield

"A little fact is worth a whole limbo of dreams."

- Ralph Waldo Emerson

"Learn, compare, collect the facts."

- Ivan Petrovich Pavlov

"The important thing in science is not so much to obtain new facts as to discover new ways of thinking about them."

- Sir William Bragg

"Insufficient facts always invites danger."

- Mr. Spock, "Star Trek"

"Let us not underrate the value of a fact. It will one day flower into a truth."

- Henry David Thoreau

"Facts do not cease to exist because they are ignored."

- Aldous Huxley

"Get your facts first, and then you can distort them as much as you please. It could probably be shown by facts and figures that there is no distinctly American criminal class except Congress."

- Mark Twain

"It is possible to store the mind with a million facts and still be entirely uneducated."

- Alec Bourne

"I don't make jokes. I just watch the government and report the facts."

- Will Rogers

"If the facts don't fit the theory, change the facts."
- Albert Einstein

"Where facts are few, experts are many."
- Donald R. Gannon

"I'm not sure I want popular opinion on my side. I've noticed those with the most opinions often have the fewest facts."
- Bethania McKenstry

"He is indebted to his memory for his jests and to his imagination for his facts.
- Richard Brinsley Sheridan

"The truth is more important than the facts."
- Frank Lloyd Wright

"The trouble with facts is that there are so many of them."
- Samuel McChord Crothers, "The Gentle Reader"

"Facts are stubborn things, but statistics are more pliable."
- Laurence J. Peter

"Every man, wherever he goes, is encompassed by a cloud of comforting convictions, which move with him like flies on a summer day."
- Bertrand Russell

"Get the facts, or the facts will get you. And when you get them, get them right, or they will get you wrong."
- Dr. Thomas Fuller

Facts

Too many business decisions are made by pushing forward without first doing due diligence. The correct order of things would be to research forces and factors first and then plan the course of action secondly. The third step is to execute the project or process, followed by benchmarking the accomplishments, outcomes and effectiveness. That benchmarking thus becomes the research phase for the next round of activities.

Gathering the facts fits into a continuum of business. Yet, what do they always cut first or bypass altogether? It's the research, which is vital to the outcomes.

The best way to build a business or a career is to investigate the facts, uncover the needs and get others to articulate what they would consider good solutions. Wise businesses employ research and customer relations techniques to stay ahead of the curve. Understanding what is being said enables further research and, with the facts in place, comes strategized organizational growth.

When you ask questions, you get answers. Sometimes, the answers are factual. Others offer reflections into how people think or feel. Still other answers contain nuggets of gold, those insights that can transform your organization into a valued success. In Corporate Strategy™, we call that Organizational Vision.

To get the best answers, one must ask the best questions, think beyond the obvious and stretch the idea process. An extended version of this concept is called a Focus Group, gleaning insights from stakeholders, prospects and target constituencies. People directly involved in the decision process may brainstorm and obtain new ideas via a Think Tank.

Facts must be plentiful and real, in order to facilitate meaningful decision making. It is the insightful interpretation of facts that makes for truly great managers and leaders.

FAILURE

"To do a great right, do a little wrong."
- William Shakespeare

"The only one who makes no mistakes is one who never does anything."
- President Theodore Roosevelt

"A life spent in making mistakes is not more honorable but more useful than a life spent doing nothing."
- George Bernard Shaw

"Tis better to have loved and lost than never to have lost at all."
- Samuel Butler

"A miss is as good as a mile."
- Proverb

"There's no success like failure. And that failure's no success at all."
- Bob Dylan

"Well, back to the old drawing board."
- Peter Arno

"The crime is not to avoid failure. The crime is not to give triumph a chance."
- Huw Wheldon

"I'm grateful for all of my problems. As each of them was overcome, it made me stronger and more able to meet those yet to come. I grew strong on my difficulties."
- J.C. Penney

"Failure...I never encountered it. All I ever met were temporary setbacks."
- J. Willard Marriott

"There's a little bit of success in every failure and a bit of failure in every success."

- O. Henry

"Life is sweetened by risks."

- Farrah Fawcett

Failure

Success and failure...it's a matter of perspectives. Out of every 10 transactions in our lives, five will be unqualified successes. One will be a failure. Two will depend upon the circumstances. If approached responsibly, they will become successful. If approached irresponsibly, they will turn into failures. Two will either be successful or will fail, based strictly upon the person's attitude.

A 90% success rate for a person with a good attitude and responsible behavior is an unbeatable percentage. There is no such thing as perfection. Continuous quality improvement means that we benchmark accomplishments and set the next reach a little further.

Throughout our lives, we search for activities, people and meaning. We venture down roads where we find success. Other activities bring us failure...from which we learn even more what to do to achieve success the next time.

We learn three times more from failure than from success. The longer that success takes to attain has a direct relationship to how long we will hold onto it. Success is easily attainable. So, why do people psyche themselves into failing more often they have to...especially when they succeed much more often than they give themselves credit for.

Learning the stumbling blocks of failure prepares one to attain true success. Fear is the biggest contributor to failure, and it can be a motivator for success. You cannot make problems go away, simply by ignoring that they exist.

Everybody fails at things for which they are not suited. The process of learning what one is best suited to do is not a failure...it is a great success. Learn from the best and the worst. People who make the biggest bungling mistakes are showing you pitfalls to avoid.

These are the most common areas where most leaders and their businesses fail:

Personal Abilities, Talents:
- Making the same mistakes more than twice, without studying the mitigating factors.
- Taking incidents out of context and mis-diagnosing situations.
- Rationalizing occurrences, after the fact.
- Appearing self-contained, therefore precluding others from wanting to help us.
- Inability to cultivate other people's support of me at the times that we needed it most.

Resources:
- Attempting projects without the proper resources to do the job well.
- Not knowing people with sufficient pull and power.
- Thinking that friends would help introduce us or help
  network to key influential people.
- Failure to learn effective networking techniques early enough in my career path.
- Inability to finely develop the powers of people participating in the networking process.

Other People:
- Accepting people at their words without questioning.
- Showing proper respect to other people and assuming that they would show or were capable of showing comparable respect to others.
- Doing favors for others without asking anything in

return... if we expected quid pro quo at a later time. • Not telling people what we wanted and then being disappointed that they did not read minds or deliver favors of their own volition.

- Befriending people who were too needy...always taking without offering to reciprocate.
- Picking the wrong causes to champion at the wrong times and with insufficient resources.
- Working with the false assumption that people want and need comparable things. Incorrectly assuming that all would pursue their agendas fairly. A better understanding of personality types, human motivations and behavioral factors would have provided insight to handle situations on a customized basis.
- Offering highly creative ideas and brain power to those who could not grasp their brilliance, especially to those who were fishing for free ideas they could then market as their own.

Circumstances Beyond Our Control:
- Working with equipment, resources and people from a source without my standards of quality control...trying to make the best of bad situations.
- Changing trends, upon which we could not capitalize but which others could.

Miscalculations:
- Incorrectly estimating the time and resources necessary to do something well.• Gettingblindsided because we did not conduct enough research.
- Failure to plan sufficiently ahead, at the right times.
- Setting sights too low. Not thinking big enough.

Timing:
- Offering advice before it was solicited.
- Feeling pressured to offer solutions before diagnosing situations properly.

- Not thinking of enough angles and possibilities... sooner.

Marketplace-External Factors:
- Not reading the opportunities soon enough.
- Not being able to spot, create or capitalize upon emerging trends at their beginnings.

Many of us make the same mistakes over and over again. That is to be expected and teaches us volumes, preparing us for success. There is no plan that is foolproof. Experience leads one to plan, learn, review and plan further.

One learns three times more from failure than success. One learns three times more clearly when witnessing and analyzing the failures of others they know or have followed. History teaches us about cycles, trends, misapplications of resources, wrong approaches and vacuums of thought. People must apply history to their own lives-situations. If we document our own successes, then these case studies will make us more successful in the future.

FAME, BRANDING, CORPORATE IMAGE

"It is a heavy burden to bear a name that is too famous."
                                                            - *Voltaire*

"Fame, if you win it, comes and goes in a minute. What is the real goal that life brings?"
        - *Lyrics from the song* "Make Someone Happy," *from the musical* "Bye Bye Birdie"

"As an adolescent I aspired to lasting fame, I craved factual certainty, and I thirsted for a meaningful vision of human life—so I became a scientist. This is like becoming an archbishop so you can meet girls."

- M. Cartmill

"Some for renown, on scraps of learning dote, and think they grow immortal as they quote."

- Edward Young, "Love of Fame"

"It is just the little touches after the average man would quit that make the master's fame."

- Orison Swett Marden

"When Alexander the Great visited Diogenes and asked whether he could do anything for the famed teacher, Diogenes replied: 'Only stand out of my light.' Perhaps some day we shall know how to heighten creativity. Until then, one of the best things we can do for creative men and women is to stand out of their light."

- John W. Gardner

"Rather than love, than money, than fame, give me truth."

- Henry David Thoreau

"He who pursues fame at the risk of losing his self is not a scholar."

- Chuang-tzu, "The Great Supreme"

"Loyalty to petrified opinion never yet broke a chain or freed a human soul."

- Mark Twain

"Wisdom alone is true ambition's aim. Wisdom the source of virtue, and of fame, obtained with labor, for mankind employed, and then, when most you share it, best enjoyed."

- Alfred North Whitehead

"Fame comes only when deserved, and then is as inevitable as destiny, for it is destiny."

- Henry Wadsworth Longfellow

Fame, Branding, Corporate Image

Organizations put disproportionate attention behind image, if the sake of business is only to become rich and famous.

In analyzing the promotional hype that one hears, some companies claim that purchasing their product is the "be all, end all" panacea for life's dilemmas. If only you will buy their version of "The Answer," then you can surely fast-forward your way to instant riches, success and an easy life.

This is not written to take swipes at responsible branding, marketing and advertising. More than 80% of what one sees and hears is clever, informative, research-based, sensibly executed and intended to orient target audiences toward marketplaces. This is written to address the bigger issue that some companies believe the hype that they are issuing.

Some companies are downright parsimonious about themselves. Some either skillfully lie to get what they think they want...or may really believe themselves to be what they hype to publics who don't know any better.

Many consumers are gullible, name-crazy and susceptible to grandiose claims. They take what is said at face value because they have not or don't care to develop abilities to discern what is hyped by others. They believe distortions faster than they believe facts, logic and reason.

This negatively impacts our society, which continually seeks button-pushing answers for life's complex problems without paying enough dues toward a truly successful life. Consumers naively believe mis-representations..to the exclusion of organizations which are more conservative, yet substantive, in their informational offerings.

Here are some of the worst "red flag" expressions. When You

Hear, Beware of False Claims!
- Our Mission.
- Family Tradition.
- Fastest Growing.
- In One Easy Lesson.
- Better.
- #1 in Sales.
- World Class.
- The Best.
- For All Your Needs.

Many of these hucksterisms are evidence of "copywriting" done by people who don't know anything about corporate vision. Their words overstate, get into the media and are accepted by audiences as fact. By default, companies have the appearance of credibility based upon mis-representations.

Companies put too much of their public persona in the hands of marketers and should examine more closely the distorted messages and partial images which they put into the cyberspace. Our culture hears and believes the hype, without looking beyond the obvious. People come to expect easy answers for questions they haven't yet taken the time to formulate.

FEAR

"Fear has many eyes and can see things underground."
- Cervantes, Don Quixote

"It is a miserable state of mind to have few things to desire and many things to fear."

- Sir Francis Bacon

"You may take the most gallant sailor, the most intrepid airman, or the most audacious soldier. Put them at a table together.

What do you get? The sum of their fears."

- Winston Churchill

"To fight a bull when you are not scared is nothing. To not fight a bull when you are scared is nothing. But, to fight a bull when you are scared, that is something."

- Manolete

"Puritanism: The haunting fear that someone, somewhere, may be happy."

- H. L. Mencken

"Courage is resistance to fear, mastery of fear - not absence of fear."

- Mark Twain

"The optimist proclaims we live in the best of all possible worlds; and the pessimist fears this is true."

- James B. Cabell

"It's the opinion of some that crops could be grown on the moon. Which raises the fear that it may not be long before we're paying somebody not to."

- Franklin P. Jones

"I do not fear computers. I fear the lack of them."

- Isaac Asimov

"You can discover what your enemy fears most by observing the means he uses to frighten you."

- Eric Hoffer

"Inferiority complex: a conviction by a jury of your fears.
Truth fears no questions. If we deny love that is given to us, if we refuse to give love because we fear pain or loss, then our lives will be empty, our loss greater. What man does not understand, he fears; and what he fears, he tends to destroy. If you fear nothing, you love nothing. If you love nothing, what

joy can there be in life?"

- Anonymous

"It's no longer socially acceptable to talk about rape as a crime of passion, boys; it's like making jokes about black people and watermelons. Unless you're from the "barefoot and pregnant" school of social relations, you should have enough sensitivity to avoid discussing extremely unpleasant violent acts in a flippant manner in front of people who must live in fear of being potential victims, or who are likely acquaintances of actual ones."

- Dave Touretzky

"It's very healthy for a young girl to be deterred from promiscuity by fear of contracting a painful, incurable disease, or cervical cancer, or sterility, or the likelihood of giving birth to a dead, blind, or brain-damage [sic] baby even ten years later when she may be happily married."

- Phyllis Schlafly

"Justice, like lightning, should ever appear To some men hope, to other mean fear."

- Jefferson Pierce

"Only a brave person is willing honestly to admit, and fearlessly to face, what a sincere and logical mind discovers."

- Rodan of Alexandria

"The final twitch of "Political Correctness" grand peur has to do with the age-old fear of antinomian beastliness, lesbians holding black masses over copies of Derrida and so forth."

- Alexander Cockburn

"To suffering there is a limit; to fearing, none."

- Sir Francis Bacon, "Of Seditions and Troubles"

"A man's ethical behavior should be based effectually on sympathy, education, and social ties; no religious basis is necessary. Man would indeed be in a poor way if he had to be restrained by fear of punishment and hope of reward after death. If people are good only because they fear punishment, and hope for reward, then we are a sorry lot indeed."

- Albert Einstein

"Power does not corrupt. Fear corrupts...perhaps the fear of a loss of power."

- John Steinbeck

"We gain strength, and courage, and confidence by each experience in which we really stop to look fear in the face... we must do that which we think we cannot." *Eleanor Roosevelt*

"One ought to seek out virtue for its own sake, without being influenced by fear or hope, or by any external influence. Moreover, that in that does happiness consist."

- Diogenes Laertius, Zeno

"The only thing we have to fear is fear itself -- nameless, unreasoning, unjustified terror which paralyzes needed efforts to convert retreat into advance."

- President Franklin D. Roosevelt

"We can gain no lasting peace if we approach it with suspicion and mistrust or with fear. We can gain it only if we proceed with the understanding, the confidence, and the courage which flow from conviction."

- President Franklin D. Roosevelt

"Don't fear change, embrace it."

- Anthony J. D'Angelo, The College Blue Book

"Everyone believes very easily whatever they fear or desire."

- Jean de La Fontaine

"Government is not reason, it is not eloquence, it is force; like fire, a troublesome servant and a fearful master. Never for a moment should it be left to irresponsible action."

- George Washington

"You can discover what your enemy fears most by observing the means he uses to frighten you."

- Eric Hoffer

"Our doubts are traitors and make us lose the good we oft might win by fearing to attempt."

- William Shakespeare

"I expect nothing. I fear no one. I am free."

- Nikos Kazantzakis

"Let us never negotiate out of fear. But let us never fear to negotiate."

- President John F. Kennedy

"Don't fear failure so much that you refuse to try new things. The saddest summary of a life contains three descriptions: could have, might have, and should have."

- Louis E. Boone

"Our deepest fear is not that we are inadequate. Our deepest fear is that we are powerful beyond measure. It is our Light, not our Darkness, that most frightens us."

- Nelson Mandela

"It shouldn't be too much of a surprise that the Internet has evolved into a force strong enough to reflect the greatest hopes and fears of those who use it. After all, it was designed to withstand nuclear war, not just the puny huffs and puffs of politicians and religious fanatics."

- Denise Caruso

"Men fear thought as they fear nothing else on earth...more than ruin, more even than death. Thought is subversive, revolutionary, destructive and terrible. Thought is merciless to privilege, established institutions and comfortable habit.

Thought looks into the pit of hell and is not afraid. Thought is great, swift, free, the light of the world, and the chief glory of man."

- Bertrand Russell

"Nothing in life is to be feared, it is only to be understood."

- Marie Curie

"We must dare to think unthinkable thoughts. We must learn to explore all the options and possibilities that confront us in a complex and rapidly changing world. We must learn to welcome and not to fear the voices of dissent. We must dare to think about unthinkable things because when things become unthinkable, thinking stops and action becomes mindless."

- James W. Fulbright

Fear

Fear is the biggest contributor to failure, and it can be a motivator for success. I use FEAR as an acronym for Find Excellence After Reflection. We are just as afraid of the things we don't know as the things in front of us. Most unknown fears turn out to not be as we had imagined.

Opportunists trade and capitalize upon fear. Several professions exist to help people get a grip on their fears. Those trying to sell will tell people what they want to hear or portray the product as being in their best interest. Some people and organizations turn others' fears into propaganda weapons for their own agendas (open or hidden). Some people and organizations take great delight in capitalizing upon the fears of others.

People are most afraid of what they don't understand. If a person scares easily, so will his neighbor. Both can know it, but they're more scared that each other will see it. After awhile, fearful people feel manipulated by others and don't know who to trust.

It is difficult to figure how people will behave when the chips are down. The definition of bravery is a person who is scared but still does what he-she has to.

═══ FUTURISM, THE FUTURE ═══

"The future ain't what it used to be."

- Yogi Berra

"Nothing's the same when you see it again."

- Cat Stevens

"The future is not a gift. It is an achievement."

- Robert F. Kennedy

"I never think of the future. It comes soon enough. The distinction between past, present, and future is only a stubbornly persistent illusion."

- Albert Einstein

"Tomorrow is another day."

- Margaret Mitchell, Gone With the Wind

"The future will one day be the present and will seem as unimportant as the present does now."

- W. Somerset Maugham

"You ain't heard nothing yet, folks."

- Al Jolson in The Jazz Singer

"You cannot fight the future. Time is on our side."

- William Gladstone

"I like the dreams of the future better that the history of the past."
- *President Thomas Jefferson*

"The fellow who can only see a week ahead is always the popular fellow, for he is looking with the crowd. But the one that can see years ahead, he has a telescope but he can't make anybody believe that he has it."
- *Will Rogers*

"The future, according to some scientists, will be exactly like the past, only far more expensive."
- *John Sladek*

"I have made good judgements in the past. I have made good judgements in the future. The future will be better tomorrow."
- *Vice President Dan Quayle*

"Everything flows and nothing abides; everything gives way and nothing stays fixed. The way up and the way down are one and the same. From out of all the many particulars comes oneness, and out of oneness come all the many particulars. A dry soul is wisest and best."
- *Heraclitus*

"So we beat on, boats against the current, borne back ceaselessly into the past."
- *F. Scott Fitzgerald*

"Modern man lives increasingly in the future and neglects the present. The future is neither ahead nor behind, on one side or another. Nor is it dark or light. It is contained within ourselves; its evil and good are perpetually within us."
- *Loren Eiseley, The Chresmologue*

"The only way to discover the limits of the possible is to go beyond them into the impossible. Any sufficiently advanced technology is indistinguishable from magic.
- *Arthur C. Clarke*, "Technology and the Future":

Hank Moore

"Where a calculator on the ENIAC is equipped with 18,000 vacuum tubes and weighs 30 tons, computers in the future may have only 1,000 vacuum tubes and perhaps weigh 1-1/2 tons."

- Popular Mechanics, March, 1949

"The best way to predict the future is to invent it."

- Alan Kay

"The trouble with our times is that the future is not what it used to be."

- Paul Valery

"The best thing about the future is that it comes one day at a time."

- President Abraham Lincoln

"I have but one lamp by which my feet are guided, and that is the lamp of experience. I know no way of judging the future but by the past. The future belongs to those who dare. Those who stare at the past have their backs turned to the future. To live for some future goal is shallow. It's the sides of the mountain that sustain life, not the top."

- Anonymous

"There is always one moment in childhood when the door opens and lets the future in."

- Graham Greene

"Run to meet the future, or it's going to run you down."
- Anthony J. D'Angelo, College Blue Book

"Upper classes are a nation's past; the middle class is its future."

- Ayn Rand

"You can never plan the future by the past."

- Edmund Burke

"Let him who would enjoy a good future waste none of his present."
- Roger Babson

"Conservation is humanity caring for the future."
- Nancy Newhall

"The empires of the future are the empires of the mind."
- Winston Churchill

"The future belongs to those who prepare for it today."
- Malcolm X

"The illiterate of the future will not be the person who cannot read. It will be the person who does not know how to learn. Man has a limited biological capacity for change. When this capacity is overwhelmed, the capacity is in future shock."
- Alvin Toffler

"In a time of drastic change it is the learners who inherit the future. The learned usually find themselves equipped to live in a world that no longer exists."
- Eric Hoffer

"The only use of a knowledge of the past is to equip us for the present. The present contains all that there is. It is holy ground; for it is the past, and it is the future."
- Alfred North Whitehead

"The future is not something we enter. The future is something we create."
- Leonard I. Sweet

"I feel that you are justified in looking into the future with true assurance, because you have a mode of living in which we find the joy of life and the joy of work harmoniously combined. Added to this is the spirit of ambition which pervades your very being, and seems to make the day's work like a happy child at play."
- Albert Einstein

"My past is my wisdom to use today. My future is my wisdom yet to experience. Be in the present because that is where life resides."

- Gene Oliver

"The most decisive actions of our life -- I mean those that are most likely to decide the whole course of our future —are, more often than not, unconsidered."

- Andre Gide

"All human situations have their inconveniences. We feel those of the present but neither see nor feel those of the future; and hence we often make troublesome changes without amendment, and frequently for the worse."

- Benjamin Franklin

"It is because modern education is so seldom inspired by a great hope that it so seldom achieves great results. The wish to preserve the past rather that the hope of creating the future dominates the minds of those who control the teaching of the young."

- Bertrand Russell

"Many people think that if they were only in some other place, or had some other job, they would be happy. Well, that is doubtful. So get as much happiness out of what you are doing as you can and don't put off being happy until some future date."

- Dale Carnegie

"To make no mistakes is not in the power of man; but from their errors and mistakes the wise and good learn wisdom for the future."

- Plutarch

"All science is concerned with the relationship of cause and effect. Each scientific discovery increases man's ability to predict the consequences of his actions and thus his ability to control future events."

- Lawrence J. Peters

"Look not mournfully into the Past. It comes not back again. Wisely improve the Present. In is thine. Go forth to meet the shadowy Future, without fear, and a manly heart."

- Henry Wadsworth Longfellow

"The greatest loss of time is delay and expectation, which depend upon the future. We let go the present, which we have in our power, and look forward to that which depends upon chance, and so relinquish a certainty for an uncertainty."

- Seneca

"At the bottom no one in life can help anyone else in life; this one experiences over and over in every conflict and every perplexity: that one is alone. That isn't as bad as it may first appear; and again it is the best thing in life that each should have everything in himself; his fate, his future, his whole expanse and world."

- Rainer Maria Rilke

Futurism, The Future

Futurism is one of the most misunderstood concepts. It is not about gazing into crystal balls or reading tea leaves. It is not about vendor "solutions" that quickly apply band-aid surgery toward organizational symptoms. Futurism is not an academic exercise that borders on the esoteric or gets stuck in the realm of hypothesis.

Futurism is an all-encompassing concept that must look at all aspects of the organization...first at the Big Picture and then at the pieces as they relate to the whole.

Futurism is a connected series of strategies, methodologies and actions which will poise any organization to weather the forces of change. It is an ongoing process of evaluation, planning, tactical actions and benchmarking accomplishments. Futurism is a continuum of thinking and reasoning skills, judicious activities, shared leadership and an accent upon ethics and quality.

I offer nine of my own definitions for the process of capturing and building a shared Vision for organizations to chart their next 10+ years. Each one gets progressively more sophisticated:

1. Futurism: what you will do and become...rather than what it is to be. What you can and are committed to accomplishing... rather than what mysteriously lies ahead.

2. Futurism: leaders and organizations taking personal responsibility and accountability for what happens. Abdicating to someone or something else does not constitute Futurism and, in fact, sets the organization backward.

3. Futurism: learns from and benefits from the past...a powerful teaching tool. Yesterdayism means giving new definitions to old ideas...giving new meanings to familiar premises. One must understand events, cycles, trends and subtle nuances because they will recur.

4. Futurism: seeing clearly your perspectives and those of others. Capitalizing upon change, rather than becoming a by-product of it. Recognizing what change is and what it can do for your organization.

5. Futurism: an ongoing quest toward wisdom. Commitments to learning, which creates knowledge, which inspire insights, which culminate in wisdom. It is more than just being taught or informed.
6. Futurism: ideas that inspire, manage and benchmark change. The ingredients may include such sophisticated business concepts as change management, crisis management and preparedness, streamlining operations, empowerment of people, marketplace development, organizational evolution and vision.

7. Futurism: developing thinking and reasoning skills, rather than dwelling just upon techniques and processes. The following concepts do not constitute Futurism by themselves: sales, technology, re-engineering, marketing, research, training, operations, administration. They are pieces of a much larger mosaic and should be seen as such. Futurism embodies thought processes that create and energize the mosaic.

8. Futurism: watching other people changing and capitalizing upon it. Understanding from where we came, in order to posture where we are headed. Creating organizational vision, which sets the stage for all activities, processes, accomplishments and goals. Efforts must be realistic, and all must be held accountable.

9. Futurism: the foresight to develop hindsight that creates insight into the future.

CHAPTER 6

Genius
Greatness, Quality
Heroes, Mentors, Role Models
History
Honesty
Hope
Human Nature

GENIUS

"Genius is 1% inspiration and 99% perspiration."
- Thomas A. Edison

"Hide not your talents. They for use were made. What's a sundial in the shade."
- Benjamin Franklin

"Genius is an infinite capacity for taking pains. The difference between genius and stupidity is that genius has its limits."
- Proverbs

"Mediocrity knows nothing higher than itself, but talent instantly recognizes genius."
- Sir Arthur Conan Doyle

"It takes people a long time to learn the difference between talent and genius, especially ambitious young men and women."
- Louisa May Alcott

"Genius does what it must, and talent does what it can."
- Owen Meredith

"The true genius is a mind of large general powers, accidentally determined to some particular direction."
- Samuel Johnson

"When a true genius appears in the world, you may know him by this sign, that the dunces are all in confederacy against him."
- Jonathan Swift

"Genius may have its limitations, but stupidity is not thus handicapped."
- Elbert Hubbard

"There's a fine line between genius and insanity. I have erased

this line."
- Oscar Levant

"But the fact that some geniuses were laughed at does not imply that all who are laughed at are geniuses. They laughed at Columbus, they laughed at Fulton, they laughed at the Wright brothers. But they also laughed at Bozo the Clown."
- Carl Sagan

"Any intelligent fool can make things bigger, more complex, and more violent. It takes a touch of genius -- and a lot of courage -- to move in the opposite direction."
- E. F. Schumacher

"Nobody in the game of football should be called a genius. A genius is somebody like Norman Einstein."
- Football quarterback Joe Theisman

"The public is wonderfully tolerant. It forgives everything except genius."
- Oscar Wilde

"Nothing in the world can take the place of persistence. Talent will not; nothing in the world is more common than unsuccessful men with talent. Genius will not; unrewarded genius is a proverb. Education will not; the world is full of educated derelicts. Persistence and determination alone are omnipotent."
- President Calvin Coolidge

"There is nothing displays the quickness of genius more than a dispute - as two diamonds, encountering, contribute to each other's luster. But perhaps the odds are against the man of taste in this particular."
- Shestone

"Genius is childhood recaptured." Bauldlaire "The author of genius does keep till his last breath the spontaneity, the ready sensitiveness, of a child, the "innocence of eye" that means so much to the painter, the ability to respond freshly and quickly to new scenes, and to old scenes as though they were new; to see traits and characteristics as though each were new-minted from the hand of God instead of sorting them quickly into dusty categories and pigeon-holing them without wonder or surprise; to feel situations so immediately and keenly that the word "trite" has hardly any meaning for him; and always to see "the correspondences between things" of which Aristotle spoke 2,000 years ago."

- *Dorothea Brande*

"Since when was genius found respectable."

- *Elizabeth Barrett Browning*

"Everyone is born with genius, but most people only keep it a few minutes."

- *Edgard Varese*

"Passion holds up the bottom of the universe and genius paints up its roof."

- *Chang Ch'ao*

"As it must not, so genius cannot be lawless; for it is even that constitutes its genius-- the power of acting creatively under laws of its own origination."

- *Samuel Taylor Coleridge*

"What makes men of genius, or rather, what they make, is not new ideas, it is that idea possessing them that what has been said has still not been said enough."

- *Eugene Delacroix*

"A man of genius is privileged only as far as he is genius. His dullness is as insupportable as any other dullness. The peril of every fine faculty is the delight of playing with it for pride. Talent is commonly developed at the expense of character, and the greater it grows, the more is the mischief. Talent is mistaken for genius, a dogma or system for truth, ambition for

greatest, ingenuity for poetry, sensuality for art."
- Ralph Waldo Emerson

"The first and last thing required of genius is the love of truth."
- Johann Wolfgang Von Goethe

"The definition of genius is that it acts unconsciously; and those who have produced immortal works, have done so without knowing how or why. The greatest power operates unseen."
- William Hazlitt

"One machine can do the work of 50 ordinary men. No machine can do the work of one extraordinary man."
- Elbert Hubbard

"A genius is the man in whom you are least likely to find the power of attending to anything insipid or distasteful in itself. He breaks his engagements, leaves his letters unanswered, neglects his family duties incorrigibly, because he is powerless to turn his attention down and back from those more interesting trains of imagery with which his genius constantly occupies his mind."
- William James

"Sometimes, indeed, there is such a discrepancy between the genius and his human qualities that one has to ask oneself whether a little less talent might not have been better."
- Carl Jung

"All the means of action—the shapeless masses—the materials - lie everywhere about us. What we need is the celestial fire to change the flint into the transparent crystal, bright and clear. That fire is genius."
- Henry Wadsworth Longfellow

"Genius without religion is only a lamp on the outer gate of a palace; it may serve to cast a gleam on those that are without while the inhabitant sits in darkness."

- Hannah More

"The only difference between a genius and one of common capacity is that the former anticipates and explores what the latter accidentally hits upon; but even the man of genius himself more frequently employs the advantages that chance presents him; it is the lapidary who gives value to the diamond which the peasant has dug up without knowing its value."

- Abbe Guillaume Raynal

"Common sense is instinct, and enough of it is genius."

- Henry Wheeler Shaw

"When a true genius appears in the world, you may know him by this sign, that the dunces are all in confederacy against him."

- Jonathan Swift

"Genius might well be defined as the ability to makes a platitude sound as though it were an original remark."

- L. B. Walton

"Let the minor genius go his light way and enjoy his life - the great nature cannot so live, he is never really in holiday mood, even though he often plucks flowers by the wayside and ties them into knots and garlands like little children and lays out on a sunny morning."

- W. B. Yeats

"So few people think. When we find one who really does, we call him a genius."

- Anonymous

"In the republic of mediocrity genius is dangerous."

- Robert G. Ingersoll

"The finest piece of mechanism in all the universe is the brain of man. The wise person develops his brain, and opens his mind to the genius and spirit of the world's great ideas. He will feel inspired with the purest and noblest thoughts that have ever animated the spirit of humanity."

- Alfred A. Montapert

"Who makes quick use of the moment is a genius of prudence."

- Johann Kaspar Lavater

"Every man who observes vigilantly, and resolves steadfastly, grows unconsciously into genius."

- Edward Bulwer-Lytton

"Whereas in art nothing worth doing can be done without genius, in science even a very moderate capacity can contribute to a supreme achievement."

- Bertrand Russell

"Every gun that is made, every warship launched, every rocket fired signifies, in the final sense, a theft from those who hunger and are not fed, those who are cold and not clothed. This world in arms is not spending money alone. It is spending the sweat of its laborers, the genius of its scientists, the hopes of its children. This is not a way of life at all in any true sense. Under the cloud of threatening war, it is humanity hanging from a cross of iron."

- President Dwight D. Eisenhower

"He who seldom speaks, and with one calm well-timed word can strike dumb the loquacious, is a genius or a hero."

- Johann Kaspar Lavater

"Talent, lying in the understanding, is often inherited; genius, being the action of reason or imagination, rarely or never."

- Samuel Taylor Coleridge

Genius

Ideas and concepts come to organizations in a variety of ways. Most have great thinkers inside and need to recognize the nuggets of gold that exist within. It is equally important to utilize consultants who really have insights and contribute original thinking, rather than those who are there to peddle off-the-shelf products and services.

The mining of golden ideas is both an art and a painstaking process. These are the seven levels of thinking and reasoning skills that lead to "genius" ideas and breakthrough concepts for a business:

1. Don't Have Them...Don't Understand That They're Essential. Some people are too consumed with just getting by. Some are preoccupied with getting more than their share from the system. Some are busy doing things without thinking them through.

2. Thinking That They're Thinking...Abdicating to Someone Else. If they believe that external forces (such as technology) will "do it all" and create the future, then their thinking skills stop here on Branch 2. Abdicating to others and reacting to situations without applying other thought processes is just acting out, not thinking out.

3. Beginning to Develop...Learning from Experiences. Trial and error. Success through learning from failures. Learning from doing, experiencing and witnessing becomes a habit.

4. Continue Adding to Their Knowledge Base. Beginning to understand how and why things happened. Noticing paradigms and patterns of behavior...in ourselves, others and situations we get ourselves into.

5. Develop Insights into Situations, Life. Maximizing the learning curve. Comprehending how to avoid pitfalls and make the most of circumstances. This leads to enlightened views of life and results in a more fulfilled usage of time and resources.

6. Develop Insights into Reasons Why, Motivations, Implications, Consequences. Learning outside one's sphere...

seeing and studying the paradigms of others. Developing the tools to function better through a Body of Knowledge.

7. Generate and Continue to Seek Wisdom. Only through progressively navigating from Branches 3-6 can one arrive at plateaus of wisdom. The truly wise person inventories what he-she does not know and accelerates the learning tracks.

═══ GREATNESS, QUALITY ═══

"A great man is always willing to be little. To be great is to be misunderstood. The essence of greatness is the perception that virtue is enough."

- Ralph Waldo Emerson

"Great deeds are usually wrought at great risks." *Herodotus*
"Be not afraid of greatness. Some are born great. Some achieve greatness. And some have greatness thrust upon them."

- William Shakespeare

"He is not great who is not greatly good."

- William Shakespeare

"Keep away from people who try to belittle your ambitions. Small people always do that, but the really great make you feel that you, too, can become great."

- Mark Twain

"A truly great man never puts away the simplicity of a child."
- Chinese proverb

"The dullard's envy of brilliant men is always assuaged by the suspicion that they will come to a bad end."

- Max Beerbohlm

"You are one of the forces of nature."

- Jules Michelet

"To be alone is the fate of all great minds...a fate deplored at times, but still always chosen as the less grievous of two evils."
- Arthur Schopenhauer

"A great city is that which has the greatest men and women."
- Walt Whitman

"The world's great men have not commonly been great scholars, nor great scholars great men."
- Supreme Court Justice Oliver Wendell Holmes

"Great men are true men, the men in whom nature has succeeded. They are not extraordinary - they are in the true order. It is the other species of men who are not what they ought to be."
- Henri-Frederic Amiel

"All great men are gifted with intuition. They know without reasoning or analysis, what they need to know."
- Alexis Carrel

"The reason why great men meet with so little pity or attachment in adversity, would seem to be this: the friends of a great man were made by his fortune, his enemies by himself, and revenge is a much more punctual paymaster than gratitude."
- C. C. Colton

"The superior man is modest in his speech but exceeds in his actions."
- Confucius

"Great men can't be ruled."
- Ayn Rand

"No great man ever complains of want of opportunity. The measure of a master is his success in bringing all men around to his opinion twenty years later."
- Ralph Waldo Emerson

"The lights of stars that were extinguished ages ago still reaches us. So it is with great men who died centuries ago, but still reach us with the radiations of their personalities."
- *Kahlil Gibran*

"There would be no great men if there were no little ones."
- *George Herbert*

"The man who is anybody and who does anything is surely going to be criticized, vilified, and misunderstood. That is part of the penalty for greatness, and every great man understands it; and understands, too, that it is no proof of greatness. The final proof of greatness lies in being able to endure continuously without resentment."
- *Elbert Hubbard*

"In our society those who are in reality superior in intelligence can be accepted by their fellows only if they pretend they are not."
- *Marya Mannes*

"No pain, no palm; no thorns, no throne; no gall, no glory; no cross, no crown."
- *William Penn*

"I believe that the first test of a truly great man is his humility. I don't mean by humility, doubt of his power. But really great men have a curious feeling that the greatness is not of them, but through them. And they see something divine in every other man and are endlessly, foolishly, incredibly merciful."
- *John Ruskin*

"It is not the greatness of a man's means that makes him independent, so much as the smallness of his wants."
- *William Cobbett*

"By constant self-discipline and self-control, you can develop greatness of character."
- *Grenville Kleiser*

"It is folly for an eminent person to think of escaping censure, and a weakness to be affected by it. All the illustrious persons of antiquity, and indeed of every age, have passed through this fiery persecution. There is no defense against reproach but obscurity; it is a kind of concomitant to greatness, as satires and invectives were an essential part of a Roman triumph."

- Joseph Addison

Greatness, Quality

Greatness and quality are not concepts that managers assign others to achieve. It is a mindset that permeates organizations from top-down as well as bottom-up.

Rather than assume all is wrong or right with an organization and take a defensive posture, management must view quality as essential to their economic survival or growth. Quality entails four concepts:

- Success is determined by conformity to requirements.
- It is achieved through prevention, not appraisal. The quality audit by objective outside communications counsel is merely the beginning of a process.
- The quality performance standard is zero defects. That means doing things correctly the first time, without wasting counter-productive time in cleaning up mistakes.
- Non-conformance is costly. Make-good efforts cost more on the back end than doing things right on the front end.

Organizations measure quality by overall involvement. It is not enough for management to endorse quality programs; they must actively participate.

Quality should be viewed as a journey, rather than a destination. It applies to service industries and manufacturing operations. Even non-profit and public sector organizations must utilize quality approaches for staff and volunteer councils/boards.

Employees must buy into the process by offering constructive input. All ideas are worthy of consideration. Life- threatening experiences (loss of business or market share, economic recession) signal the urgency for the team to collaborate.

Empowerment of employees means they accept the challenges and consequences. They must view the company as a consumer would...being as discerning about buying their own services as they are about fine dining, premium clothing, gifts for friends, a car or a home.

What if we were all paid based upon customer perceptions of our service? That would make each of us more attentive to what we offer and whether our value is correctly perceived.

Each member of an organization must view himself/herself as having customers. Each must be seen as a profit center and as having something valuable to contribute to the overall group. Each is a link that lets down the whole chain by failing to uphold their part.

What is missing in most organizations is the willingness to move forward, not the availability of information or room/ desire for improvement. Willingness requires complete and never-ending commitment by management. The first time the organization tolerates anything less than 100%, it is on the road back to mediocrity.

The most common pitfalls toward success include:
- Taking a piecemeal approach to quality.
- Thinking that quality applies to some other department, company or industry, not your own.
- Thinking that you are already doing things "the quality way."
- Failing to address structural flaws that fuel the problems.
- Focusing upon esoteric techniques, rather than true

reasons for instilling quality.
- Saying that something is being done when it is not.
- Failing to engage customers and suppliers into the process.
- Failing to emphasize training.
- Setting goals that are too low.
- Communicating poorly with the organization and its publics. Without employee communications, suggestion boxes, publications, training videos, speeches and other instruments, the company is fooling itself and its customers about the commitment to quality. Without good communication from the outset, the program will never be understood and accepted.

Quality improvement is the only action that can simultaneously win the support of customers, employees, investors, media and the public. Productivity translates to profitability in an advantageous climate in which to function.

Research shows the by-product costs of poor quality are high for any business, up to 40%. Lack of attentiveness to quality has cost the United States its global marketplace dominance. Other nations preceded the U.S. in adopting the quality process and overtook our nation in many areas.

In 1981, more than 70% of U.S. automobiles realized defects within six months of purchase. That figure has now dropped below 40%, compared with just under 30% in Japanese cars. Had quality been a focus in Detroit years earlier, then the obvious would not have transpired.

The Japanese have always viewed quality as a national issue...not just an individual company matter. The real victim of America's late entry into the quality process was every employee whose livelihood was endangered. Consumers did not worry; they simply bought goods and services elsewhere.

Greatness via competitiveness has many dimensions:
- Production efficiency became America's focus by the 1950's.
- Marketing's importance was fully embraced in the 1960's. Marketing departments deal most often and

immediately with the side-effects of poor quality.

- The 1970's brought the first wave of strategic planning. Without mapping a course, how can any organization reach a destination?
- The 1980's brought us the quality process...which is the bow that wraps a package containing the other three elements. At the start of the decade, many executives viewed the quality process with indifference or fear. By decade's end, virtually all (92%) agreed that quality is the main prescription for survival.

Though quality is one element of competitiveness, it cannot cover defects in the other areas. The quality audit by objective outside communications counsel can also examine the production, marketing and strategic planning functions.

Companies must place demands upon their own organizations to embrace customer service tenets. Satisfied customers talk to others...encouraging them to buy based upon quality of the company. Dissatisfied customers will aggressively discourage higher numbers of prospects from buying.

The mark of any professional is the manner in which he/she corrects mistakes. Most often, this means correcting misperceptions about company attitude, rather than the condition of goods. The faster the correction, the better the level of satisfaction.

Greatness and quality are the sum of impressions made upon the customer. Especially during tough economic times, investment in a quality program is not costly. In the long-run, it pays. Anyone who is unwilling to spend for quality is hastening their company's decline.

HEROES, MENTORS, ROLE MODELS

"We can't all be heroes because somebody has to sit on the

curb and clap as they go by."
- Will Rogers

"There are new words now that excuse everybody. Give me the good old days of heroes and villains. the people you can bravo or hiss. There was a truth to them that all the slick credulity of today cannot touch."
- Bette Davis

"Nurture your mind with great thoughts; to believe in the heroic makes heroes."
- Benjamin Disraeli

"True courage is not the brutal force of vulgar heroes, but the firm resolve of virtue and reason."
- Alfred North Whitehead

"Show me a hero, and I will write you a tragedy."
- F. Scott Fitzgerald

Heroes, Mentors, Role Models

For many years, I have mentored CEOs and top executives on how to be leaders for their companies, in their communities and on wider stages.
One of the earliest exercises that I give them is my Mentorship Survey, asking them to inventory the top 10-20 things that have meant the most to their careers. I ask them to recall the ideas, their age at the time of learning, from whom they learned the applicable lessons and the long-term implications for these teachings.

What one learns from this fruitful exercise is that one-third of our great lessons came from formal teachers, mentors and role models. One-third of our great lessons came from people who were not considered heroes, and, by watching their mistakes and shortcomings, we became wiser for it. The final third of our great lessons came from within ourselves...for we realize, after all, that we must be our own role model and spread those insights to others.

I grew up and spent my early professional years around the entertainment world and the political arena. Having met many celebrities, entertainers and media heroes, I know that raw talent does not directly translate to business savvy and people skills.

One of my first career idols was Dick Clark, a man who is smart and accomplished in many facets. He had just debuted on "American Bandstand." I was in the fifth grade and started working at a radio station, determined to be Texas' answer to Dick Clark.

A mentor reminded me that none of us should go through life as a carbon copy of someone else. We can admire and embody their qualities but must carve out a uniqueness all our own. Good advice from a 24-year-old Bill Moyers, who stands for me as an ever-contemporary role model.

Corporate executives do not get a rulebook when the job title is awarded. They are usually promoted on the basis technical expertise, team player status, loyalty and perceived long- term value to the company. They are told to assume a role and then draw upon their memory bank of role models.

Top executives were not taught to be leaders. They had few role models in equivalent positions. Thus, they get bad advice from the wrong consultants. In the quest to be a top business leader, one quickly reviews how poorly corporate executives were portrayed to the mass culture.

This progression of statements, validations and commitments is the premise of this book, which is just the   same approach utilized when I work with corporate clients on strategizing and visualizing their future:

- Examine where you came from.
- Retread old knowledge.
- Apply teachings to today.
- Honestly evaluate your path to progress thus far.

- Affix responsibilities, goals and benchmarks to all intended progress.
- Find creative new ways to approach and conduct business.
- Proceed with zeal, commitment, creative instinct and boundless energy.
- Achieve and reflect upon successes.
- Learn three times more from failure than success.
- Plan to achieve and succeed in the future.
- Never stop researching, planning, executing and evaluating.
- Benchmarks of one phase, project or series of events drive the research and planning for the next phase.
- Futurism is not an esoteric concept. It is about planning to weather storms of the future and is directly applicable to daily success.

HISTORY

"History repeats itself."

- Proverb

"History will be kind to me, for I intend to write it."
- Sir Winston Churchill

"More than any other time in history, mankind faces a crossroads. One path leads to despair and utter hopelessness. The other, to total extinction. Let us pray we have the wisdom to choose correctly."

- Woody Allen

"The Beat Goes On."

- Sonny Bono

"It is not the neutrals or lukewarms who make history." *Adolph*
- Hitler

"All things from eternity are of like forms and come round in a circle."

- Marcus Aurelius

"History is philosophy teaching by examples."

- Dionsius of Halicarnassus

"Man is a history-making creature who can neither repeat his past nor leave it behind."

- W.H. Auden

"Nothing has really happened until it has been recorded."

- Virginia Woolf

"History is an endless repetition of the wrong way of living."

- Lawrence Durrell

"History is nothing more than a tableau of crimes and misfortunes."

- Voltaire

"The history of science is everywhere speculative. It is a marvelous history. It makes you proud to be a human being."

- Karl R. Popper

"If Beethoven had been killed in a plane crash at the age of 22, it would have changed the history of music⊠ and of aviation."

- Tom Stoppard

"For four-fifths of our history, our planet was populated by pond scum."

- J.W. Schopf

"Whenever we read the obscene stories, the voluptuous debaucheries, the cruel and torturous executions, the unrelenting vindictiveness, with which more than half the bible is filled, it would seem more consistent that we called it the word of a demon than the Word of God. It is a history of

wickedness that has served to corrupt and brutalize mankind."
- Thomas Paine

"Happy are the people whose annals are blank in history books."
- Thomas Carlyle

"Human history becomes more and more a race between education and catastrophe."
- H. G. Wells

"All humanity is passion; without passion, religion, history, novels, art would be ineffectual."
- Honore De Balzac

"From their experience or from the recorded experience of others (history), men learn only what their passions and their metaphysical prejudices allow them to learn." *Aldous Huxley*
"A page of history is worth a pound of logic."
- Supreme Court Justice Oliver Wendell Holmes

"There is a history in all men's lives."
-- William Shakespeare

"A true history of human events would show that a far larger proportion of our acts as the results of sudden impulses and accident, than of the reason of which we so much boast."
- Albert Cooper

"If, after all, men cannot always make history have meaning, they can always act so that their own lives have one."
- Albert Camus

"In studying the history of the human mind one is impressed again and again by the fact that the growth of the mind is the widening of the range of consciousness, and that each step forward has been a most painful and laborious achievement. One could almost say that nothing is more hateful to man than to give up even a particle of his unconsciousness. Ask those who have tried to introduce a new idea!"

- Carl Jung

"We are living the events which for centuries to come will be minutely studied by scholars who will undoubtedly describe these days as probably the most exciting and creative in the history of mankind. But, preoccupied with our daily chores, our worries and personal hopes and ambitions, few of us are actually living in the present."

- Lawrence K. Frank

"The history of human opinion is scarcely more than the history of human errors."

- Voltaire

"Poetry comes nearer to vital truth than history."

- Plato

"Books are the carriers of civilization. Without books, history is silent, literature dumb, science crippled, thought and speculation at a standstill. I think that there is nothing more opposed to poetry, to philosophy, to life itself than this incessant business."

- Henry David Thoreau

"In history as in life it is success that counts. Start a political upheaval and let yourself be caught, and you will hang as a traitor. But place yourself at the head of a rebellion and gain your point, and all future generations will worship you as the Father of their Country."

- Hendrik Van Loon

"In all our efforts to provide advantages, we have actually produced the busiest, most competitive, highly pressured and over-organized generation in our history."

- Eda J. Le Shan

"History teaches us that men and nations behave wisely once

they have exhausted all other alternatives."

- Abba Eban

"The Holocaust was an obscene period in this century's history. People that are really very weird can get into sensitive positions and have a tremendous impact on history."

- Vice President Dan Quayle

"One of the lessons of history is that nothing is often a good thing to do and always a clever thing to say."

- Will Durant

"Hegel was right when he said that we learn from history that man can never learn anything from history."

- George Bernard Shaw

"History is the short trudge from Adam to atom."

- Leonard Louis Levinson

"History is the version of past events that people have decided to agree upon."

- Napoleon Bonaparte

History

From history, I've learned that there's nothing more permanent than change. For everything that changes, many things remain the same. The art of living well is to meld the changeable dynamics with the constants and the traditions. The periodic reshuffling of priorities, opportunities and potential outcomes represents business planning at its best.

One learns three times more from failure than from success. By studying and reflecting upon the events of the past and the shortcomings of others, then we create strategies for meeting the challenges of the future.

In business, we must learn lessons from the corporate crises, the also-rans and the conditions which controlled the history. Some of those lessons that we could well learn came from these watershed events:

- The Civil War. This is a classic and tragic case of two sides fighting for causes and not fully understanding the other side's motivations. The South saw slavery as an economic factor and the only system of labor management they had ever known. The North saw opportunities to champion humanity issues, underlying the threat of insurgence within our own nation. Neither side fully articulated its issues, nor sought to negotiate before hostilities broke out. This war caused severe rifts in U.S. society for another 100 years.

- Shift from an Agricultural to an Industrial Economy.

- Prohibition. Take something away from consumers, and say that the action is in their best interest. They'll want the commodity even more. The great lengths that people went to getting their liquor fixes enabled organized crime to gain major footholds in America. The legislation that created Prohibition was wrong, and that action by a few spawned the gangster era, which became big business in America. Congress finally recounted after untollable damage was done.

- The Great Depression. Economics are a series of ebbs and flows. Failure to anticipate and to prepare for the next drop and to expect that the good times will never cease is foolhardy. Failure to exercise crisis management after the crash and to restore stability in judicious ways caused the Depression to drag on. It was a World War that finally pulled America out of its greatest economic slump. Lessons from the Great Depression should have been applied during the high-riding days of technology stocks and a stock market that over-hyped so much. The dotcom bust and Enronesque debacles could have been avoided if lessons from the Great Depression had been learned, updated and utilized.

- Diversity in the Workplace.

- Shift from an Industrial to an Information Economy.

- Watergate...bringing about more accountability by the public sector..

- The DotCom Bust. As stated above, analogies from the

Great Depression to the dotcom crash were many. Too many tech companies did not feel as though corporate protocols of the older companies applied to them. Shortcuts were taken. The media unfairly crowned superficial darlings, such as Enron. Regulators had relaxed standards. Common practice in investment communities was to over-hype stock potential, without seeing who was truly at the switches of these companies. Had the scandals not triggered public outcry when they did, this chain of events could have led to another Great Depression.

- Enron and other corporate scandals, bringing about reforms, ethics and higher corporate accountability.
- Changing management styles. Customer Focused Management is the prevailing orientation, and companies must adapt.

HONESTY

"Honesty is the best policy."

- President George Washington

"Honesty is hardly ever heard...and mostly what I need from you."

- Billy Joel

"A little sincerity is a dangerous thing, and a great deal of it is absolutely fatal."

- Oscar Wilde

"An honest man's word is as good as his bond." Proverb "If you do not tell the truth about yourself, you cannot tell it about other people."

- Virginia Woolf

"To be honest, as this world goes, is to be one man picked out of ten thousand. To be direct and honest is not safe. Though I am not naturally honest, I am so sometimes by chance."

- William Shakespeare

"The best measure of a man's honesty isn't his income tax return. It's the zero adjust on his bathroom scale."
- Arthur C. Clarke

"There is no kind of dishonesty into which otherwise good people more easily and frequently fall than that of defrauding the government."
- Benjamin Franklin

"It is inaccurate to say that I hate everything. I am strongly in favor of common sense, honesty and common decency. This makes me forever ineligible for public office."
- H.L. Mencken

"Honesty is the best image."
- Ziggy (Tom Wilson)

"Honesty pays, but it doesn't seem to pay enough to suit some people."
- F. M. Hubbard

"Honesty is a good thing, but it is not profitable to its possessor unless it is kept under control."
- Don Marquis

"Honesty is the best policy - when there is money in it."
- Mark Twain

"You must pay for conformity. All goes well as long as you run with conformists. But you, who are honest men in other particulars, know that there is alive somewhere a man whose honesty reaches to this point also, that he shall not kneel to false gods, and, on the day when you meet him, you sink into the class of counterfeits."
- Ralph Waldo Emerson

"It was a grand trait of the old Roman that with him one and the same word meant both honor and honesty."
- Advance

"Make yourself an honest man, and then you may be sure that there is one rascal less in the world."

- Thomas Carlyle

"Nothing more completely baffles one who is full of trick and duplicity than straightforward and simple integrity in another. A knave would rather quarrel with a brother knave than with a fool, but he would rather avoid a quarrel with one honest man than with both. He can combat a fool by management and address, and he can conquer a knave by temptations. But the honest man is neither to be bamboozled nor bribed."

- C. C. Colton

"That which is won ill, will never wear well, for there is a curse attends it which will waste it. The same corrupt dispositions which incline men to sinful ways of getting, will incline them to the like sinful ways of spending."

- M. Henry

"Would you want to do business with a person who was 99% honest?"

- Sidney Madwed

"The honest man must be a perpetual renegade, the life of an honest man a perpetual infidelity. For the man who wishes to remain faithful must take himself perpetually unfaithful to all the continual, successive, indefatigable, renascent errors."

- Charles Peguy

"We must make the world honest before we can honestly say to our children that honesty is the best policy."

- George Bernard Shaw

"I hope I shall possess firmness and virtue enough to maintain what I consider the most enviable of all titles, the character of an honest man."

- President George Washington

"How frequently are the honesty and integrity of a man

disposed of by a smile or a shrug. How many good and generous actions have been sunk into oblivion by a distrustful look, or stamped with the imputation of bad motives, by a mysterious and seasonable whisper!"

- Sterne

"Concentration is my motto...first honesty, then industry, then concentration."

- Andrew Carnegie

HOPE

"Hope is a walking dream."

- Aristotle

"Hope is the physician of each misery. Never deprive someone of hope...it may be all they have. A drowning man will clutch at a straw. Hope for the best. It is a long lane that has no turning. While there's life, there's hope."

- Proverbs

"The miserable have no other medicine but only hope."

- William Shakespeare

"He that lives upon hope will die fasting."

- Benjamin Franklin

"If it were not for hopes, the heart would break."

- Thomas Fuller

"More than any other time in history, mankind faces a crossroads. One path leads to despair and utter hopelessness. The other, to total extinction. Let us pray we have the wisdom to choose correctly."

- Woody Allen

"Yesterday I was a dog. Today I'm a dog. Tomorrow I'll probably

still be a dog. Sigh! There's so little hope for advancement."
- Snoopy

"We forfeit three-fourths of ourselves to be like other people. Every nation ridicules other nations, and all are right. Everyone takes the limits of his own vision for the limits of the world."
- Arthur Schopenhauer

"A man's ethical behavior should be based effectually on sympathy, education, and social ties; no religious basis is necessary. Man would indeed be in a poor way if he had to be restrained by fear of punishment and hope of reward after death."
- Albert Einstein

"As Mankind becomes more liberal, they will be more apt to allow that all those who conduct themselves as worthy members of the community are equally entitled to the protections of civil government. I hope ever to see America among the foremost nations of justice and liberality."
- President George Washington

"Hope is nature's veil for hiding truth's nakedness."
- Alfred Bernhard Nobel

"There is hopeful symbolism in the fact that flags do not wave in a vacuum."
- Arthur C. Clarke

"Gratitude is merely the secret hope of further favors."
- Francious de la Rochefoucauld

"Unless commitment is made, there are only promises and hopes...but no plans."
- Peter Drucker

"To deny we need and want power is to deny that we hope to be effective."
- Liz Smith

"One ought to seek out virtue for its own sake, without being influenced by fear or hope, or by any external influence. Moreover, that in that does happiness consist."
- Diogenes Laertius, Zeno

"If I had to choose between betraying my country and betraying my friend, I hope I should have the guts to betray my country."
- Forster

"To cherish what remains of the Earth and to foster its renewal is our only legitimate hope of survival."
- Wendell Berry

"Hope is a state of mind, not of the world. Hope is not the same as joy that things are going well, or willingness to invest in enterprises that are obviously heading for success, but rather an ability to work for something because it is good."
- Vaclav Havel

"Most of the important things in the world have been accomplished by people who have kept on trying when there seemed to be no hope at all."
- Dale Carnegie

"Make no little plans; they have no magic to stir men's blood and probably will themselves not be realized. Make big plans; aim high in hope and work, remembering that a noble, logical diagram once recorded will not die."
- Daniel Burnham

"Nothing average ever stood as a monument to progress. When progress is looking for a partner, it doesn't turn to those who believe they are only average. It turns instead to those who are forever searching and striving to become the best they possibly can. If we seek the average level, we cannot hope to achieve a high level of success. Our only hope is to avoid being a failure."
- Lou Vickery

"Take hope from the heart of man, and you make him a beast of prey."

- Ouida (Marie Louise de la Ramee)

"Life may not be the party we hoped for, but while we're here we should dance."

- Anonymous

"It is from numberless diverse acts of courage and belief that human history is shaped. Each time a man stands up for an ideal, or acts to improve the lot of others, or strikes out against injustice, he sends forth a tiny ripple of hope, and crossing each other from a million different centers of energy and daring, those ripples build a current that can sweep down the mightiest walls of oppression and resistance."

- Robert F. Kennedy

"I can endure my own despair but not another's hope."

- William Walsh

"Reconciliation should be accompanied by justice, or it will not last. While we all hope for peace it shouldn't be peace at any cost but peace based on principle, on justice."

- Corazon Aquino

"You are not here merely to make a living. You are here in order to enable the world to live more amply, with greater vision, with a finer spirit of hope and achievement. You are here to enrich the world, and you impoverish yourself if you forget the errand."

- President Woodrow Wilson

"Hope, like faith, is nothing if it is not courageous; it is nothing if it is not ridiculous."

- Thornton Wilder

"What then have I done? What, except yield to a natural feeling, inspired by beauty, sanctioned by virtue and kept at all times within the bounds of respect. It's innocent expression

prompted not by hope but by trust."
- Vicomte de Valmont, Les Liaisons Dangereuses

"Make no little plans; they have no magic to stir men's blood...
Make big plans...aim high in hope and work."
- Daniel H. Burnham

"We promise according to our hopes and perform according
to our fears."
- Anonymous

"At 20, a man is full of fight and hope. He wants to reform the
world. When he is 70, he still wants to reform the world, but he
knows he can't."
- Clarence Darrow

"To be 70 years young is sometimes far more cheerful and
hopeful than to be 40 years old."
- Supreme Court Justice Oliver Wendell Holmes

"It is not for man to rest in absolute contentment. He is born
to hopes and aspirations as the sparks fly upward, unless he
has brutified his nature and quenched the spirit of immortality
which is his portion."
- Robert Southey

"Despair is vinegar from the wine of hope."
- Austin O'Malley

"Oft expectation fails, and most oft where most it promises;
and oft it hits where hope is coldest; and despair most sits."
- William Shakespeare

"Let us think of education as the means of developing our
greatest abilities, because in each of us there is a private hope
and dream which, fulfilled, can be translated into benefit for
everyone and greater strength for our nation."
- President John F. Kennedy

"It is because modern education is so seldom inspired by a great hope that it so seldom achieves great results. The wish to preserve the past rather that the hope of creating the future dominates the minds of those who control the teaching of the young."

- Bertrand Russell

"Few things in the world are more powerful than a positive push. A smile. A word of optimism and hope. A 'you can do it' when things are tough."

- Richard M. DeVos

"If I had to choose between betraying my country and betraying my friend, I hope I should have the guts to betray my country."

- E. M. Forster

"The building of a perfect body crowned by a perfect brain, is at once the greatest earthly problem and grandest hope of the race."

- Dio Lewis

"I hope I shall possess firmness and virtue enough to maintain what I consider the most enviable of all titles, the character of an honest man."

- President George Washington

"Before you give up hope, turn back and read the attacks that were made on Lincoln."

- Bruce Barton

"My country owes me nothing. It gave me, as it gives every boy and girl, a chance. It gave me schooling, independence of action, opportunity for service and honor. In no other land could a boy from a country village, without inheritance or influential friends, look forward with unbounded hope."

- President Herbert Hoover

"Hope is both the earliest and the most indispensable virtue inherent in the state of being alive. If life is to be sustained hope must remain, even where confidence is wounded, trust impaired."

- Erik H. Erikson

"Hope is the last thing that dies in man; and though it be exceedingly deceitful, yet it is of this good use to us, that while we are traveling through life it conducts us in an easier and more pleasant way to our journey's end."

- Francois, Duc De La Rochefoucauld

"Hope is the companion of power, and mother of success; for who so hopes strongly has within him the gift of miracles."

- Samuel Smiles

"We are living the events which for centuries to come will be minutely studied by scholars who will undoubtedly describe these days as probably the most exciting and creative in the history of mankind. But preoccupied with our daily chores, our worries and personal hopes and ambitions, few of us are actually living in the present."

- Lawrence K. Frank

"But peace does not rest in the charters and covenants alone. It lies in the hearts and minds of all people. So let us not rest all our hopes on parchment and on paper, let us strive to build peace, a desire for peace, a willingness to work for peace in the hearts and minds of all of our people. I believe that we can. I believe the problems of human destiny are not beyond the reach of human beings."

- President John F. Kennedy

"Prejudice is the conjurer of imaginary wrongs, strangling truth, overpowering reason, making strong men weak and weak men weaker. God give us the large hearted charity which beareth all things, believe all things, hope all things, endure all things, which 'thinks no evil.'"

- Macduff

"Every gun that is made, every warship launched, every rocket fired signifies, in the final sense, a theft from those who hunger and are not fed, those who are cold and not clothed. This world in arms is not spending money alone. It is spending the sweat of its laborers, the genius of its scientists, the hopes of its children. This is not a way of life at all in any true sense. Under the cloud of threatening war, it is humanity hanging from a cross of iron."

- Dwight D. Eisenhower

"The hopes of the Republic cannot forever tolerate either undeserved poverty or self-serving wealth."

- President Franklin D. Roosevelt

"The poor and the affluent are not communicating because they do not have the same words. When we talk of the millions who are culturally deprived, we refer not to those who do not have access to good libraries and bookstores, or to museums and centers for the performing arts, but those deprived of the words with which everything else is built, words that opens doors. Children without words are licked before they start. The legion of the young wordless in urban and rural slums, 8-10 years old, do not know the meaning of hundreds of words which most middle-class people assume to be familiar to much younger children. Most of them have never seen their parents read a book or a magazine, or heard words used in other than rudimentary ways related to physical needs and functions. Thus is cultural fallout caused the vicious circle of ignorance and poverty reinforced and perpetuated. Children deprived of words become school dropouts; dropouts deprived of hope behave delinquently. Amateur censors blame delinquency on reading immoral books and magazines, when the inability to read anything is the basic trouble."

- Peter S. Jennison

"People wish to be settled. It is only as far as they are unsettled that there is any hope for them."

- Ralph Waldo Emerson

"A man can do what he wants, but not want what he wants."
- Arthur Schopenhauer

Hope

We can wish that things would change. Embracing change is the next step. Planning for the future follows next. Measuring that plan for results and accountability must indeed follow.

Every business needs a qualified mentor to see that hope translates into actions.

══════ HUMAN NATURE ══════

"Men and melons are hard to know."
- Benjamin Franklin

"The nature of men is always the same. It is their habits that separate them."
- Conficius

"Man is the only animal that blushes or needs to. If you pick up a starving dog and make him prosperous, he will not bite you. This is the principal difference between dog and man."
- Mark Twain

"We are usually the best men when in the worst health. It is almost impossible to smile on the outside without feeling better on the inside. It is a pleasure to give advice, humiliating to need it, normal to ignore it. Too many people confine their exercise to jumping to conclusions, running up bills, stretching the truth, bending over backward, lying down on the job, sidestepping responsibility and pushing their luck."
- Proverbs

"Most human beings have an almost infinite capacity for taking things for granted."

- Aldous Huxley

"Scenery is fine, but human nature is finer."

- John Keats

"A rarer spirit never did steer humanity. Give us faults to make us men."

- William Shakespeare

"Moral indignation is mostly 2% moral, 48% indignation and 50% envy."

- Vittorio De Sica

"Only the brave know how to forgive; it is the most refined and generous pitch of virtue human nature can arrive at."

- Sterne

"It is human nature to hate him whom you have injured."

- Tacitus

"Drinking without being thirsty and making love at any time, Madame, are the only things that distinguish us from other animals."

- Beaumarchis

"The sufferers parade their miseries, tear lint from their bruises, reveal their indictable crimes, that you may pity them. They like sickness, because physical pain will extort some show of interest from bystanders, as we have seen children, who, finding themselves of no account when grown people come in, will cough till they choke, to draw attention."

- Ralph Waldo Emerson

"Nature is trying very hard to make us succeed, but nature does not depend on us. We are not the only experiment." R. - Buckminster Fuller

"The man of power is ruined by power, the man of money by

money, the submissive man by subservience, the pleasure seeker by pleasure." Hermann Hesse "Human nature is not of itself vicious."

- Thomas Paine

"It is often easier to fight for one's principles that to live up to them."

- Adlai E. Stevenson

"Laughter, while it lasts, slackens and unbraces the mind, weakens the faculties and causes a kind of remissness and dissolution in all the powers of the soul. If we consider the frequent reliefs we receive from it and how often it breaks the gloom which is apt to depress the mind and damp our spirits, one would take care not to grow too wise for so great a pleasure of life."

- Joseph Addison

Human Nature

It is customary to follow your gut and proceed along. Businesses cannot steer themselves just by coasting. Planning and strategy move that human nature into actionable results.

Each year, one-third of the U.S. Gross National Product goes toward cleaning up problems, damages and otherwise high costs of doing either nothing or doing the wrong things.

On the average, it costs six times the investment of preventive strategies to correct business problems (compounded per annum and exponentially increasing each year). In some industries, the figure is as high as 20 times... six is the mean average. This is a premise that was detailed in one of my other books, "The High Cost of Doing Nothing."

The old adage says: "An ounce of prevention is worth a pound of cure." One pound equals 16 ounces. In that scenario, one pound of cure is 16 times more mostly than an ounce of prevention.

Human beings as we are, none of us do everything perfectly on the front end. There always must exist a learning curve. Research shows that we learn three times more from failures than from successes. The mark of a quality organization is how it corrects mistakes and prevents them from recurring.

Running a profitable and efficient organization means effectively remediating damage before it accrues. Processes and methodologies for researching, planning, executing and benchmarking activities will reduce that pile of costly coins from stacking up.

CHAPTER 7

Ideas
Knowledge
Language, Semantics, Labels
Laziness
Leadership
Lies

IDEAS

"All great ideas are dangerous."

- Oscar Wilde

"An idea isn't responsible for the people who don't believe it."
- Don Marquis

"You can't shoot an idea."
- Presidential candidate Thomas E. Dewey

"All good things which exist are the fruit of originality."
- John Stuart Mill

"The hours of a wise man are lengthened by his ideas."
- Joseph Addison

"Paradoxes are useful to attract attention to ideas."
- Mandell Creighton

"Man is ready to die for an idea, provided that idea is not quite clear to him."

- Paul Eldridge

"A society made up of individuals who were all capable of original thought would probably be unendurable. The pressure of ideas would simply drive it frantic."

- H.L. Mencken

"The link between ideas and action is rarely direct. There is almost always an intermediate step in which the idea is overcome. De Tocqueville points out that it is at times when passions start to govern human affairs that ideas are most obviously translated into political action. The translation of ideas into action is usually in the hands of people least likely to follow rational motives. Hence, it is that action is often the nemesis of ideas, and sometimes of the men who formulate them. One of the marks of the truly vigorous society is the ability to dispense with passion as a midwife of action - the ability to pass directly from thought to action."

- Eric Hoffer

"Some men never seem to grow old. Always active in thought, always ready to adopt new ideas, they are never chargeable with foggyism. Satisfied, yet ever dissatisfied, settled, yet ever unsettled, they always enjoy the best of what is, are the first to find the best of what will be."

- William Shakespeare

"Everyone is in business for himself, for he is selling his services, labor or ideas. Until one realizes that this is true he will not take conscious charge of his life and will always be looking outside himself for guidance."

- Sidney Madwed

"But you can catch yourself entertaining habitually certain ideas and setting others aside; and that, I think, is where our personal destinies are largely decided."

- Alfred North Whitehead

"What makes men of genius, or rather, what they make, is not new ideas, it is that idea - possessing them - that what has been said has still not been said enough."

- Eugene Delacroix

"It is useless to send armies against ideas."

- Georg Brandes

"There is only one way in which a person acquires a new idea; by combination or association of two or more ideas he already has into a new juxtaposition in such a manner as to discover a relationship among them of which he was not previously aware."

- Francis A. Carter

"Neither man or nation can exist without a sublime idea."

- Feodor Dostoyevsky

"We are prisoners of ideas."

- Ralph Waldo Emerson

"Men who accomplish great things in the industrial world are the ones who have faith in the money producing power of ideas."

- Charles Fillmore

"Whenever I hear people talking about "liberal ideas," I am always astounded that men should love to fool themselves with empty sounds. An idea should never be liberal; it must be vigorous, positive, and without loose ends so that it may fulfill its divine mission and be productive. The proper place for liberality is in the realm of the emotions."

- Johann Wolfgang Von Goethe

"A new and valid idea is worth more than a regiment and fewer men can furnish the former than command the latter."
- Supreme Court Justice Oliver Wendell Holmes

"An idea, to be suggestive, must come to the individual with the force of revelation."

- William James

"It isn't easy for an idea to squeeze itself into a head filled with prejudice. Too many people run out of ideas long before they run out of words."

- Proverbs

"First comes thought; then organization of that thought, into ideas and plans; then transformation of those plans into reality. The beginning is in your imagination."

- Napolean Hill

"The finest mechanism in all the universe is the brain of man. The wise person develops his brain and opens his mind to the genius and spirit of the world's great ideas. He will feel inspired with the purest and noblest thoughts that have ever animated the spirit of humanity."

- Alfred A. Montapert

Ideas

These are the stages in the evolution of ideas, concepts and philosophies:

1. Information, Data. There is more information available now than ever before. Most of it is biased and slanted by vendors with something to sell. There exists much data, without interpretation. Technology purveys information but cannot do the analytical thinking.

2. Perception. Appearance of data leads to initial perceptions—usually influenced by the media in which the information exists. To many people and organizations, perception is reality because they do not delve any further, thus, learning stops at this point.

3. Opinion. Determined more by events-processes than words. Verbal statements are more important when people are suggestible and need interpretation from a credible source. Does not anticipate emergencies...only reacts to them. Many perceptions and opinions are self-focused and affected by self-esteem. Once self-interest becomes involved, opinions do not change easily.

4. Ideas and Beliefs. Formulated ideas emerge, as people-organizations learn to hold their own outside their shells. Two-way communication ensues...opinion inputs and outputs craft ideas and beliefs. As people become more aware of their own learning, they tally their inventory of knowledge. Patterns of beliefs emerge, based upon education, experiences and environment.

5. Systems of Thought and Ideologies. Insights start emerging at this plateau. Connect beliefs with available resources and personal expertise. Measure results and evaluate outcomes of activities, using existing opinion, ideas and beliefs. Actions are taken which benchmark success and accountability to stakeholders.

6. Core value. Shaped by ideas, beliefs, systems of thought and ideologies. Becomes what the person or organization stands for. Has conviction, commitment and ownership. Able to change and adapt. Behavioral modification from the old ways of thinking has transpired.

7. Company-Career-Life Vision. An informed and enlightened plateau that few achieve. Able to disseminate information, perceptions and opinions for what they really are. Wisdom focused...an evolving flow of philosophies. A quest to employ ideologies and core values for benefit of all in the organization. Committed to and thriving upon change.

KNOWLEDGE

"The only good is knowledge and the only evil is ignorance."
- Socrates

"If money is your hope for independence you will never have it. The only real security that a man will have in this world is a reserve of knowledge, experience, and ability."
- Henry Ford

"Religion is the masterpiece of the art of animal training, for it trains people as to how they shall think."
- Arthur Shopenhauer

"My views and feelings are in favor of the abolition of war—and I hope it is practicable, by improving the mind and morals of society, to lessen the disposition to war; but of its abolition I despair."
- Thomas Jefferson

Knowledge

Amassing a Body of Knowledge, which leads to Wisdom, is a long and enjoyable process. It is the first step toward a career-life Strategy, which evolves into a Vision. Using a corporate analogy, a Mission Statement accounts for less than 1% of a Strategic Plan, which constitutes only 20% of a Corporate Visioning Program.

Business evolution is an amalgamation of thoughts, technologies, approaches and commitment of the people, asking such tough questions as:

1. What would you like for you and your organization to become?
2. How important is it to build an organization, rather than spend time managing conflict?
3. Who are the customers?
4. Do successful corporations operate without a strategy-vision?
5. Do you and your organization presently have a strategy-vision?
6. Are businesses really looking for creative ideas? Why?
7. If no change occurs, is the research and self-reflection worth anything?

Most of us learned about business (which is a compendium of life relationships) "in the streets." Today's business leaders entered and pursued careers without a a strategic plan or service manual.

Failure to prepare for the future spells certain death for businesses and industries in which they function. The same analogies apply to personal lives, careers and Body of Work. Greater business awareness and heightened self awareness are compatible and part of a holistic journey of growth.

None of us can escape those pervasive influences that have affected our lives...which I describe as The Learning Tree. Like sponges, we absorb information and perceptions of life that have helped mold our business and personal relationships.

LANGUAGE, SEMANTICS, LABELS

"Whereof one cannot speak, thereof one must be silent. In order to draw a limit to thinking, we should have to think both sides of this limit. Uttering a word is like striking a note on the keyboard of the imagination."

- Ludwig Wittgenstein, Philosophical Investigations

"I have no doubt that in reality the future will be vastly more surprising than anything I can imagine. Now my own suspicion is that the universe is not only queerer than we suppose, but queerer than we can suppose." J. B. S. Haldane, "Possible Worlds and Other Papers""We cut nature up, organize it into concepts, and ascribe significances as we do, largely because we are parties to an agreement to organize it in this way - an agreement that holds through our speech community and is codified in the patterns of our language."

- Benjamin Lee Whorf

"The belief that words have a meaning of their own account is a relic of primitive word magic, and it is still a part of the air we breathe in nearly every discussion."

- Charles K. Ogden

"Even the most scientific investigator in science, the most thoroughgoing Positivist, cannot dispense with fiction; he must at least make use of categories, and they are already fictions, analogical fictions, or labels, which give us the same pleasure as children receive when they are told the "name" of a thing."

- Havelock Ellis

Language, Semantics, Labels

Organizations are accustomed to looking at concepts and practices one way at a time. Clinging to obsolete definitions and viewpoints has a way of perpetuating companies into downward spirals.

By viewing from others' viewpoints on life, we find real nuggets of gold with which to redefine organizations. Companies that adopt new viewpoints and defy their conventional definitions will create new opportunities, organizational effectiveness, marketplaces and relationships.

As a Big Picture strategist, I encourage new ways of thinking about old processes, including those which brought past and enduring successes. Symbolic are these phrase definitions which I have created for familiar business words.

The purpose of any business is not just to make money. It is to be just:
- Committed to customers.
- Respectful of employees.
- Successful enough to grow, pay its dues and continue growing.
- Upholding standards of quality and commitment.
- Focused through everything else we back to our customers.

Too often, one hears about what goes wrong in business relationships. From our viewpoint, if business is conducted honorably and professionally, then profitability and success flow from doing the right things...not from pursuing false goals.

The best successes are earned and learned. We should not take fortune for granted. Business track records are garnered by going the distance, reading the trends and continually changing. As the years go by, one continues paying dues. Learning, experiencing and evaluating is the best process to achieve lasting success. The best dues yield nuggets of wisdom that couldn't have been earned any other way.

The smartest person is the one who knows what he/she does not know. With maturity comes the quest to learn more, understand the factors and apply newly acquired insights to higher purposes. The person who commits to a path of professional development never stops achieving...and profitably impacts his-her business relationships.

Language is food for the mind. Browse a dictionary, and you'll create new ideas. Word play is fun. Technology cannot take the place of human communication; it can only add to it. Every opportunity should be taken to enhance literacy skills of employees and entire organization. The language of success is initially found in a dictionary.

LAZINESS

"Idle men are dead all their life long."

- Thomas Fuller

"Tis the voice of the sluggard. I heard him complain, 'You have waked me too soon. I must slumber again.'"

- Isaac Watts

"Efficiency is intelligent laziness."

- David Dunham

"Laziness is nothing more than the habit of resting before you get tired."

- Jules Renard

"Sloth makes all things difficult, but industry, all things easy. He that rises late must trot all day, and shall scarce overtake his business at night. Laziness travels so slowly that poverty soon overtakes him."

- Benjamin Franklin

"A great deal of laziness of mind is called liberty of opinion."

- Anonymous

Laziness

What often happens as a result of unplanned growth is that the original business gets shoved to the back burner. The new business thrust gets proportionately more than its share of attention. Capitalization is stretched beyond limits, and operations advance in a cash-poor mode.
Morale wavers and becomes uneven, per operating unit and division. Attempts to bring consistency and uniformity drive further wedges into the operation. The company expands and subsequently contracts without strategic planning.

These are the defeating signs for growth companies:

1. Systems are not in place to handle rapid growth... perhaps never were.
2. Their only interest is in booking more new business, rather than taking care of what they've already got.
3. Management is relying upon financial people as the primary source of advice, while ignoring the rest of the picture (90%).
4. Team empowerment suffers. Morale is low or uneven.
5. Commitment from workers drops because no corporate culture was created or sustained.
6. Customer service suffers during fast-growth periods.
7. They have to back-pedal and recover customer confidence by doing surveys. Even with results of deteriorating customer service, growth-track companies pay lip service to really fixing their own problems.

People do not have the same Vision as the company founder... who has likely not taken enough time to fully develop a Vision and obtain buy-in from others.

Company founder remains arrogant and complacent, losing touch with marketplace realities and changing conditions.

Everything we are in business stems from what we've been taught or not taught. A career is all about devoting resources to amplifying talents and abilities, with relevancy toward a viable end result.

LEADERSHIP

"A leader is a dealer in hope."

- Napoleon Bonaparte

"A president's hardest task is not to do what is right but to know what is right."

- President Lyndon B. Johnson

"When you're leading, don't talk."

- Thomas E. Dewey

"A leader who doesn't hesitate before he sends his nation into battle is not fit to be a leader."

- Golda Meir

"Leadership and learning are indispensable to each other."
- President John F. Kennedy

"An empowered organization is one in which individuals have the knowledge, skill, desire, and opportunity to personally succeed in a way that leads to collective organizational success."

- Stephen R. Covey

"Men make history, and not the other way around. In periods where there is no leadership, society stands still. Progress occurs when courageous, skillful leaders seize the opportunity to change things for the better."
- President Harry S Truman

"Leadership should be born out of the understanding of the needs of those who would be affected by it."
- Marian Anderson

"Leadership has a harder job to do than just choose sides. It must bring sides together."
- Reverend Jesse Jackson

"Jingshen is the Mandarin word for spirit and vivacity. It is an important word for those who would lead, because above all things, spirit and vivacity set effective organizations apart from those that will decline and die."
- James L. Hayes, Memos for Management: Leadership

"The only real training for leadership is leadership."
- Anthony Jay

"I start with the premise that the function of leadership is to produce more leaders, not more followers."
- Ralph Nader

"Whether a man is burdened by power or enjoys power; whether he is trapped by responsibility or made free by it; whether he is moved by other people and outer forces or moves them -- this is of the essence of leadership."
- Theodore H. White, The Making of the President

"You do not lead by hitting people over the head. That's assault, not leadership."
- President Dwight D. Eisenhower

"Leadership is practiced not so much in words as in attitude and in actions."

- Harold Geneen

"Good leadership consists in showing average people how to do the work of superior people."

- John D. Rockefeller

"There are no office hours for leaders."

- Cardinal James Gibbons

"A leader never sets himself above followers except in carrying responsibilities."

- Jules Ormont

Leadership

The biggest problem with business stems from the fact that management and company leadership come from one small piece of the organizational pie. Filling all management slots with financial people, for example, serves to limit the organizational strategy and focus. They all hire like-minded people and frame every business decision from their micro perspective.

The ideal executive has strong leadership skills first. He or she develops organizational vision and sets strategies. Leaders should reflect a diversity of niche focus, guaranteeing that an overall balance is achieved. Those with ideologies, strategies, process upholding and detail focus are all reflected. The best management team looks at the macro, rather than just the niche micro.

None of us was born with sophisticated, finely tuned senses and highly enlightened viewpoints for life. We muddle through, try our best and get hit in the gut several times. Thus, we learn, amass knowledge and turn most experiences into an enlightened life-like perspective that moves us "to the next tier." Such a perspective is what makes seasoned executives valuable in the business marketplace.

Many people, however, stay in the "muddling through" mode and don't acquire seasoning. They "get by" with limited scope and remain complacent in some kind of security. As their clueless increases, they sink through the following seven numbers, like they would fall into a well.

Life has a way of forcing the human condition to change. Due to circumstances, people start "cluing in." By that point, substantial career potential has been lost. Much damage cannot be recovered. Therefore, many people likely will stay on safe tracks and will rarely ride the engine to glory.

At some point, each of us takes ownership for our lives, careers and accomplishments. Events which may necessitate or inspire this to happen could include:
- A recognition that the old methods are not working.
- Successive failures via the old ways of doing things.
- Financial failures or the monetary incentive to rapidly create or change plans of action.
- Loss of one or more loved ones (by death). Loss of parents causes one to grow up exponentially.
- Loss of one or more valued relationships, because they were not properly nurtured or were blatantly neglected.
- A pattern of scapegoating others for one's own problems and issues.
- There is no choice but to change the modus operandi.
- Loss of substantial numbers of opportunities, customers, employees and market share.
- A "wake up call" of any type.

People are hard pressed to recall the exact moment when their value systems emerged. That's a steady process and a circuitous journey.

The most effective leaders accept that change is 90% positive and find reasons and rationale to embrace change. They see how change relates to themselves, realizing that the process of mastering change and turning transactions into a series of win-win propositions constitutes the real meaning of life.

Leadership is learned and synthesized daily. Knowledge is usually amassed through unexpected sources. Any person's commitment toward leadership development and continuing education must include honest examination of his-her life skills. Training, reading and pro-activity are prescribed.

LIES

"Little white lies are like little white rabbits. They multiply big."
- Charlie Chan

"He who multiplies riches multiplies cares."
- Benjamin Franklin

"White lies always introduce others of a darker complexion."
- William S. Paley

"Oh what a tangled web we weave, when first we practice to deceive."
- Sir Walter Scott

"Without lies, humanity would perish of despair and boredom."
- Anatole France

"By the time the child can draw more that scribble, by the age of four or five years, an already well-formed body of conceptual knowledge formulated in language dominates his memory and controls his graphic work. Drawings are graphic accounts of essentially verbal processes. As an essentially verbal education gains control, the child abandons his graphic efforts and relies almost entirely on words. Language has first spoilt drawing and then swallowed it up completely."
- Karl Buhler

"I have heard it said that the first ingredient of success - the earliest spark in the dreaming youth - if this; dream a great dream."

- John Alan Appleman

"Some families can trace their ancestors back three hundred years, but can't tell you where their children were last night. What lies behind us and what lies before us are tiny matters compared to what lies within us."

- Anonymous

"There is no one, says another, whom fortune does not visit once in his life; but when she does not find him ready to receive her, she walks in at the door, and flies out at the window."

- Montesquieu

"Freedom, then, lies only in our innate human capacity to choose between different sorts of bondage, bondage to desire or self esteem, or bondage to the light that lightens all our olives."

- Sri Madhava

"Man has three friends on whose company he relies. First, wealth which goes with him only while good fortune lasts. Second, his relatives; they go only as far as the grave, leave him there. The third friend, his good deeds, go with him beyond the grave."

- The Talmud

"When of a gossiping circle it was asked, 'What are they doing?' The answer was, 'Swapping lies."

- Richard Brinsley Sheridan

"The man who is anybody and who does anything is surely going to be criticized, vilified, and misunderstood. That is part of the penalty for greatness, and every great man understands it; and understands, too, that it is no proof of greatness. The final proof of greatness lies in being able to endure continuously without resentment."

- Elbert Hubbard

"Hope is both the earliest and the most indispensable virtue inherent in the state of being alive. If life is to be sustained hope must remain, even where confidence is wounded, trust impaired."

- Erik H. Erikson

"Falsehood is never so successful as when she baits her hook with truth, and no opinions so fatally mislead us, as those that are not wholly wrong; as no watches so effectually deceive the wearer as those that are sometimes right."

- C. C. Colton

"Lies are usually caused by undue fear of men."

- Hasidic saying

"Sin has many tools, but a lie is the handle which fits them all."

- Oliver Wendell Holmes, Jr.

"He who has not a good memory should never take upon himself the trade of lying."

- Michel De Montaigne

"Falsehood has an infinity of combinations. Truth has only one mode of being."

- Jean-Jacques Rousseau

"A liar begins with making falsehood appear like truth, and ends with making truth itself appear like falsehood."

- William Shenstone

"Clever liars give details, but the cleverest don't. The more you talk to yourself, the more apt you are to lie. A fellow who says he has never told a lie has just told one. It is easier to believe a lie that one has heard many times than to believe a fact that no one has heard before."

- Anonymous

"Good manners and good morals are sworn friends and fast

allies."

- C. A. Bartol

"Our minds are like our stomachs; they are whetted by the change of their food, and variety supplies both with fresh appetites."

- Quintilian

"Prejudice squints when it looks, and lies when it talks."

- Duchess de Abrantes

"There are pauses amidst study, and even pauses of seeming idleness, in which a process goes on which may be likened to the digestion of food. In those seasons of repose, the powers are gathering their strength for new efforts; as land which lies fallow recovers itself for tillage."

- J. W. Alexander

"Learn from the earliest days to insure your principles against the perils of ridicule; you can no more exercise your reason if you live in the constant dread of laughter, that you can enjoy your life if you are in the constant terror of death."

- Sydney Smith

"In oneself lies the whole world and if you know how to look and learn, the door is there and the key is in your hand. Nobody on earth can give you either the key or the door to open, except yourself."

- J. Krishnamarti

"Set priorities for your goals. A major part of successful living lies in the ability to put first things first. Indeed, the reason most major goals are not achieved is that we spend our time doing second things first."

- Robert J. McKain

"According to Democritus, truth lies at the bottom of a well, the water of which serves as a mirror in which objects may be reflected. I have heard, however, that some philosophers, in seeking for truth, to pay homage to her, have seen their own image and adored it instead."

- Charles Richter

"It is only necessary to make war with five things; with the maladies of the body, the ignorances of the mind, with the passions of the body, with the seditions of the city and the discords of families."

- Pythagoras

"I have been thinking that I would make a proposition to my Republican friends...that if they will stop telling lies about the Democrats, we will stop telling the truth about them."

- Adlai Stevenson

"There are three kinds of lies: lies, damned lies, and statistics."
- Benjamin Disraeli

"Time flies like an arrow. Fruit flies like a banana."
- Lisa Grossman

"I know the answer! The answer lies within the heart of all mankind! The answer is 12? I think I'm in the wrong building."
- Charles Schulz

"Truth is beautiful, without doubt; but so are lies."
- Ralph Waldo Emerson

"Organized crime in America takes in over forty billion dollars a year and spends very little on office supplies."
- Woody Allen

"My problem lies in reconciling my gross habits with my net income."
- Errol Flynn

"Everybody lies, but it doesn't matter because nobody listens."
- Nick Diamos

"Americans detest all lies except lies spoken in public or printed lies."

- Ed Howe

"Wars teach us not to love our enemies, but to hate our allies."
- W. L. George

"The chief value of money lies in the fact that one lives in a world in which it is overestimated."

- H. L. Mencken

"It's all right to have butterflies in your stomach. Get them to fly in formation."

- Dr. Rob Gilbert

"What lies behind us and what lies before us are tiny matters compared to what lies within us."

- Ralph Waldo Emerson

"I always remember an epitaph which is in the cemetery at Tombstone, Arizona. It says: 'Here lies Jack Williams. He done his damnedest.' I think that is the greatest epitaph a man can have - When he gives everything that is in him to do the job he has before him. That is all you can ask of him and that is what I have tried to do."

- President Harry S. Truman

"Let me tell you the secret that has lead me to my goal. My strength lies solely in my tenacity."

- Louis Pasteur

"When the conduct of men is designed to be influenced, persuasion, kind unassuming persuasion, should ever be adopted. It is an old and true maxim that 'a drop of honey catches more flies than a gallon of gall.' So with men. If you would win a man to your cause, first convince him that you are his sincere friend. Therein is a drop of honey that catches his heart, which, say what he will, is the great highroad to his reason, and which, once gained, you will find but little trouble in convincing him of the justice of your cause, if indeed that cause is really a good one."

- President Abraham Lincoln

"Real, constructive mental power lies in the creative thought that shapes your destiny, and your hour-by-hour mental conduct produces power for change in your life. Develop a train of thought on which to ride. The nobility of your life as well as your happiness depends upon the direction in which that train of thought is going."

- Laurence J. Peter

"Those that think it permissible to tell white lies soon grow color blind."

- Austin O'Malley

"Things won are done. Joy's soul lies in the doing."

- William Shakespeare

Lies

We live in a cliche oriented society. Without thinking, people say canned comments, often inventing contexts in which to frame them. Relationships of all kinds are cliched to death. Creativity often gives way to the familiar and the trite.

It is amazing how often business discussions are derailed by cliches. Grasping for descriptive words, executives generalize with platitudes. Most commonly, without conscious intent, cliches are utilized as control mechanisms to shut down new, innovative discussion.

Here, then, are the Great Lies. As you read these categorized lists, think of when and where you first heard them. Think of situations where people who spoke these lines shot their companies in the foot. Associate with people whose management styles were self-defeating.

Business Meeting Lies...
- I can do all of that.
- There's nothing they've got that I can't have...and deserve. I've done that for years.
- I can be anything I want to be.
- You can do anything that you set your heart to do.
- They're not up to my standards anyway.
- I could have had that job if I had wanted it.
- That's beneath me. I don't have to do that.
- You want it? It's yours for the taking.
- I'm building for the future. Tomorrow is the day when it will happen.

Tacit Resignation...
- I really don't have a master plan.
- I'm still trying as hard as I can.
- I'll get there someday.
- Que sera, sera. Whatever will be will be.
- There are too many things keeping me from accomplishing my objectives.
- That's life.
- Another day, another dollar. Oh, well...
- You know how accountants (or any other profession) are! If it isn't one thing, it's another.
- I can't help the way that I am.

Someone Else Has a Plan...
- The future will create itself.
- Everything happens for a reason.
  - They must be doing something right. Why quibble with a winner?
- That's someone else's problem.
- I don't have all the answers.
- Let George do it.
- Why tamper with success? It's worked so far.
- If you don't know, I can't tell you.

Once you rethink and reflect upon business lies heard, you will begin fashioning retorts to negative comments heard. It is when we recognize generalities as self-defeating and positively reframe, then proactive change and continuous quality improvement will naturally occur.

CHAPTER 8

Management
Mediocrity
Memory
Mistakes
Negotiations, Compromise
Opportunity

MANAGEMENT

"Management is nothing more than motivating other people."
- Lee Iacocca

"In the modern world of business, it is useless to be a creative original thinker unless you can also sell what you create. Management cannot be expected to recognize a good idea unless it is presented to them by a good salesman."
- David M. Ogilvy

"A place for everything and everything in its place."
- Isabella Mary Beeton

"Jingshen is the Mandarin word for spirit and vivacity. It is an important word for those who would lead, because above all things, spirit and vivacity set effective organizations apart from those that will decline and die."
- James L. Hayes, "Memos for Management: Leadership"

"It's all very well in practice, but it will never work in theory."
- French management saying

"So much of what we call management consists in making it difficult for people to work. Management means, in the last analysis, the substitution of thought for brawn and muscle, of knowledge for folklore and superstition, and of cooperation for force. Management is doing things right; leadership is doing the right things. Management by objectives works if you first think through your objectives. Ninety percent of the time you haven't."
- Peter F. Drucker

"Good plans shape good decisions. That's why good planning helps to make elusive dreams come true."
- Lester R. Bittel, The Nine Master Keys of Management

"Good management is the art of making problems so interesting and their solutions so constructive that everyone wants to get to work and deal with them."

- Paul Hawken

"A little tact and wise management may often evade resistance, and carry a point, where direct force might be in vain."

- Author Unknown

"Nothing more completely baffles one who is full of trick and duplicity than straightforward and simple integrity in another. A knave would rather quarrel with a brother knave than with a fool, but he would rather avoid a quarrel with one honest man than with both.."

- C. C. Colton

Management

Research tells us that 92% of all problems in organizations stem from poor management decisions. Having studied, worked with and mentored many managers over the years, I've concluded that few had sufficient management training up to that point. The system simply does not train executives, nor managers, nor leaders.

In the period that predated scientific management, the Captain of Industry style prevailed. Prior to 1885, titans of industry were rulers, as had been the land barons of earlier years. Policies were dictated, and people complied without question. Some captains were notoriously ruthless. Others like Rockefeller, Carnegie and Ford channeled their wealth and power into giving back to the communities. It was a grandiose era of self-made millionaires and the people who toiled in their mills.

From 1885-1910, the labor movement gathered steam. Negotiations and collective bargaining focused on conditions for the workers and physical plant environments. This was an era when American business had fully segued from an agricultural-based economy to an industrial-based reality.

As a counterbalance for industrial reforms and strength of unions, a Hard Nosed style of leadership was prominent from 1910-1939. This was management's attempt to take stronger hands, recapture some of the Captain of Industry style and build solidity into an economy plagued by the Depression. This is an important phase to remember because it is the mindset of addictive organizations, chronicled in Chapter 3.

The Human Relations style of management flourished from 1940-1964. Under it, people were managed. Processes were managed as collections of people. Employees began having greater says in the execution of policies. Yet, the rank and file employees at this point were not involved in creating policies, least of all strategies and methodologies.

Management by Objectives came into vogue in 1965 and was the prevailing leadership style until 1990. In this era, business started embracing formal planning. Other important components of business (training, marketing, research, team building and productivity) were all accomplished according to goals, objectives and tactics.

In 1991, Customer Focused Management became the standard. Customer focused management is dedicated to providing members with an opportunity to identify, document and establish best practices through benchmarking to increase value, efficiencies, and profits.
Corporate leaders are products of the eras in which they grew up. They formed their value systems by the music,
movies, TV and literature of the era. For most top corporate leaders, to understand their orientation is to fully understand the 1950s and 1960s. That's a concept that I call Pop Culture Wisdom...which is another book in itself.

Most corporate leaders are a management generation or two behind. Those who matured in the era of the Human Relations style of management were still clinging to value systems of

Hard Nosed. They were not just "old school." They went to the school that was torn down to build the old school. That's Enron and their ilk in a nutshell.

Similarly, baby boomer executives who were educated in the Management by Objectives era were still recalling value systems of their parents' generation before it. Baby boomers with a Depression-era frugality and value of tight resources are more likely to take a bean counter-focused approach to business. That's my concern that financial-only focus without regard to other corporate dynamics bespeaks of hostile takeovers, ill-advised rollups and corporate raidering for books of business.

Younger executives who were educated and came of age during the early years of Customer Focused Management had still not comprehended and embraced its tenets. They also mirrored pop culture icons. Sadly, many young people saw J.R. Ewing as a role model and further his modes of operation to this day. Thus, the dotcom bust. In a nutshell, the "new school" of managers did not think that corporate protocols and strategies related to them. The game was to just write the rules as they rolled along. Such thinking always invites disaster, as so many of their stockholders found out.

Given that various management eras are still reflected in the New Order of Business, we must learn from each and move forward.

MEDIOCRITY

"Only mediocrity can be trusted to be at its best."
                                                            - *Max Beerbohm*

"Some men are born mediocre. Some men achieve mediocrity. And some men have mediocrity thrust upon them."
                                                            - *Joseph Heller, Catch-22*

"The world is a republic of mediocrities and always was."
- Thomas Carlyle

"It isn't evil that is ruining the earth, but mediocrity. The crime is not that Nero played while Rome burned, but that he played badly."
- Ned Rorem

"There is real magic in enthusiasm. It spells the difference between mediocrity and accomplishment."
- Dr. Norman Vincent Peale

"Mediocrity does not see higher than itself. But talent instantly recognizes the genius."
- Sir Arthur Conan Doyle

"The essential element of successful strategy is that it derives its success from the differences between competitors with a consequent difference in their behavior. Ordinarily, this means that any corporate policy and plan which is typical of the industry is doomed to mediocrity. Where this is not so, it should be possible to demonstrate that all other competitors are at a distinct disadvantage."
- Bruce Henderson

"Anybody who accepts mediocrity—in school, on the job, in life—is a person who compromises, and when the leader compromises, the whole organization compromises."
- Charles Knight

"People who have accomplished work worthwhile have had a very high sense of the way to do things. They have not been content with mediocrity. They have not confined themselves to the beaten tracks; they have never been satisfied to do things just as others so them, but always a little better. They always pushed things that came to their hands a little higher up, this little farther on, that counts in the quality of life's work. It is constant effort to be first-class in everything one attempts that

conquers the heights of excellence."
- Orison Swett Marden

"Solitude, the safeguard of mediocrity."
- Ralph Waldo Emerson

"In the republic of mediocrity genius is dangerous."
- Robert G. Ingersoll

"Minds of moderate caliber ordinarily condemn everything which is beyond their range."
- Francois, Duc De La Rochefoucauld

"Mediocrity is not allowed to poets, either by the gods or man."
- Horace

MEMORY

"Memory is the thing you forget with."
- Alexander Chase

"Everyone complains of his memory, but no one complains of his judgment."
- Duc de la Rochefoucauld, 17th Century French writer

"The nice thing about having memories is that you can choose."
- William Trevor

"There is no monument dedicated to the memory of a committee."
- Lester J. Pourciau

"One of the keys to happiness is a bad memory."
- Rita Mae Brown

"A person is never happy except at the price of some ignorance."
- Anatole France

"Why is it that our memory is good enough to retain the least triviality that happens to us and yet not good enough to recollect how often we have told it to the same person?"
- La Rochefoucauld

"A lot of people mistake a short memory for a clear conscience."
- Doug Larson

"Happiness is nothing more than good health and a bad memory."
- Albert Schweitzer

"Memory feeds imagination."
- Amy Tan

"The secret of a good memory is attention, and attention to a subject depends upon our interest in it. We rarely forget that which has made a deep impression on our minds."
- Tryon Edwards

"The palest ink is better than the best memory."
- Chinese Proverb

"One must have a good memory to be able to keep the promises one makes."
- Nietzsche

"Own only what you can carry with you; know language, know countries, know people. Let your memory be your travel bag."
- Alexander Solzhenitsyn

"By the time the child can draw more that scribble, by the age of four or five years, an already well-formed body of conceptual knowledge formulated in language dominates his memory and controls his graphic work. Drawings are graphic accounts of essentially verbal processes. As a verbal education gains control, the child abandons his graphic efforts and relies almost entirely on words. Language has first spoilt drawing and then swallowed it up completely."

- Karl Buhler

"Adults interfere with a natural development of the child's motor, visual, mental and artistic abilities when they try to influence the child's work in the early years. The adult's brain has accumulated much more visual and artistic memory than the child's. There can be no true meeting of adult and child mind unless the adult knows how the child's mind functions in art."

- Rhoda Kellogg

"We are students of words; we are shut up in schools, and colleges, and recitation rooms, for ten or fifteen years, and come out at last with a bag of wind, a memory of words, and do not know a thing."

- Ralph Waldo Emerson

"Nothing fixes a thing so intensely in the memory as the wish to forget it. He who is not very strong in memory should not meddle with lying. He who has not a good memory should never take upon himself the trade of lying."

- Michel De Montaigne

"If you want to win friends, make it a point to remember them. If you remember my name, you pay me a subtle compliment; you indicate that I have made an impression on you. Remember my name and you add to my feeling of importance."

- Dale Carnegie

"Our memories are card indexes consulted, and then put back in disorder by authorities whom we do not control."

- Cyril Connolly

"Memory depends very much on the perspicuity, regularity, and order of our thoughts. Many complain of the want of memory, when the defect is in the judgment; and others, by grasping at all, retain nothing."

- Thomas Fuller

"We can remember minutely and precisely only the things which never really happened to us."

- Eric Hoffer

"Memory tempers prosperity, mitigates adversity, control youth, and delights old age."

- Firmianus Lactantius

"What we learn with pleasure we never forget."

- Alfred Mercier

"Lulled in the countless chambers of the brain, our thoughts are linked by many a hidden chain; awake but one, and in, what myriads rise!"

- Alexander Pope

"Memory is not wisdom; idiots can by rote repeat volumes. Yet what is wisdom without memory?"

- Martin Tupper

"So live that your memories will be part of your happiness. Nothing improves the memory more than trying to forget."

- Anonymous

"A poet ought not to pick nature's pocket. Let him borrow, and so borrow as to repay by the very act of borrowing.
Examine nature accurately, but write from recollection, and trust more to the imagination than the memory."

- Samuel Taylor Coleridge

"He is a benefactor of mankind who contracts the great rules of life into short sentences, that may be easily impressed on the memory, and so recur habitually to the mind."

- Samuel Johnson

Memory

People are interesting combinations of the old, the new, the tried and the true. Individuals and organizations are more resilient than they tend to believe. They've changed more than they wish to acknowledge. They embrace innovations, while keeping the best traditions.

When one reflects at changes, he-she sees directions for the future. Change is innovative. Customs come and go....some should pass and others might well have stayed with us.
There's nothing more permanent than change. For everything that changes, many things stay the same. The quest of life is to interpret and adapt that mixture of the old and new. People who fight change have really changed more than they think.

The past is an excellent barometer for the future. I call that Yesterdayism. One can always learn from the past, dust it off and reapply it. I call that Lessons Learned but Not Soon Forgotten. Living in the past is not good, nor is living in the present without wisdom of the past.

Trends come and go...the latest is not necessarily the best. Some of the old ways really work better...and should not be dismissed just because they are old or some fashionable trend of the moment looks better.

When we see how far we have come, it gives further direction for the future. Ideas make the future happen. Technology is but one tool of the trade. Futurism is about people, ideas and societal evolution, not fads and gimmicks. The marketplace tells us what they want, if we listen carefully. We also have an obligation to give them what they need.

In olden times, people learned to improvise and "make do." In modern times of instantaneous disposability, we must remember the practicalities and flexibilities of the simple things and concepts.

MISTAKES

"Two wrongs do not make a right."

- Proverb

"Mistakes...we all make them. That's why we have erasers."

- James Garner, as Bret Maverick

"The weak have one weapon...the errors of those who think they are strong."

- Georges Bidault

"What we call experience is often a dreadful list of ghastly mistakes."

- J. Chalmers Da Costa

"To err is human, to forgive, divine." Alexander Pope "The physician can bury his mistakes, but the architect can only advise his client to plant vines."

- Frank Lloyd Wright

"As soon as we started programming, we found to our surprise that it wasn't as easy to get programs right as we had thought. Debugging had to be discovered. I can   remember the exact instant when I realized that a large part of my life from then on was going to be spent in finding mistakes in my own programs."

- Maurice Wilkes

"Experience...is simply the name we give our mistakes. Nowadays most people die of a sort of creeping common sense, and discover when it is too late that the only things one never regrets are one's mistakes."

- Oscar Wilde

"A life spent making mistakes is not only more honorable, but more useful than a life spent doing nothing."

- George Bernard Shaw

"If I had to live my life again, I'd make the same mistakes, only sooner."

- Tallulah Bankhead

"We're all capable of mistakes, but I do not care to enlighten you on the mistakes we may or may not have made."

- Vice President Dan Quayle

"When I woke up this morning my girlfriend asked me, 'Did you sleep good?' I said 'No, I made a few mistakes.'"

- Stephen Wright

"An expert is a person who has made all the mistakes that can be made in a very narrow field."

- Niels Bohr

"If I had my life to live over, I'd make more mistakes. I'd relax, limber up and be sillier than I have been this trip. I would take fewer things seriously. I would take more chances, climb more mountains and swim more rivers. I would eat more ice cream and less beans. I would perhaps have more actual trouble, but I'd have fewer imaginary ones. I'm one of those people who live sensibly and sanely hour after hour, day after day. I've had my moments, and if I had to do it over again, I'd have more of them. I'd try to have nothing else...just moments, one after another, instead of living so many years ahead of each day. I've been one of those persons who never goes anywhere without a thermometer, hot water bottle, raincoat and parachute. If I had to do it again, I would travel lighter that I have. I would start barefoot earlier in the spring and stay that way later in the fall. I would go to more dances. I would ride more merry-go-rounds. I would pick more daisies."

- Nadine Stair

"No matter what we have come through, or how many perils we have safely passed, or how many imperfect and jagged - in some places perhaps irreparably - our life has been, we cannot in our heart of hearts imagine how it could have been different. As we look back on it, it slips in behind us in orderly array,

Hank Moore

and, with all its mistakes, acquires a sort of eternal fitness, and even, at times, of poetic glamour."

- Randolph Silliman Bourne

"Men heap together the mistakes of their lives and create a monster they call destiny."

- John Oliver Hobbes

"Mistakes are a great educator when one is honest enough to admit them and willing to learn from them."

- Anonymous

"No man ever became great or good except through many and great mistakes."

- W. E. Gladstone

"Show us a man who never makes a mistake and we will show you a man who never makes anything. The only men who are past the danger of making mistakes are the men who sleep at Greenwood."

- H. L. Wayland

"None are too wise to be mistaken, but few are so wisely just as to acknowledge and correct their mistakes, and especially the mistakes of prejudice."

- Barrow

"To make no mistakes is not in the power of man; but from their errors and mistakes the wise and good learn wisdom for the future."

- Plutarch

"The man who trusts men will make fewer mistakes that he who distrusts them."

- Conte Di Camillo Benso Cavour

"Would you like me to give you a formula for success? It's quite simple, really. Double your rate of failure. You are thinking of failure as the enemy of success. But it isn't as all. You can be discouraged by failure or you can learn from it. So go ahead and make mistakes. Make all you can. Because, remember that's where you will find success."

- Thomas J. Watson

"I've got to keep breathing...it'll be my worst business mistake if I don't."

- Nathan Meyer Rothschild

"The higher up you go, the more mistakes you're allowed. Right at the top, if you make enough of them, it's considered to be your style."

- Fred Astaire

"You will make all kinds of mistakes; but as long as you are generous and true, and also fierce, you cannot hurt the world or even seriously distress her."

- Sir Winston Churchill

"The only way to even approach doing something perfectly is through experience, and experience is the name everyone gives to their mistakes."

- Oscar Wilde

"The Athenians, alarmed at the internal decay of their Republic, asked Demosthenes what to do. His reply: "Do not do what you are doing now."

- Joseph Ray

"Do not look where you fell, but where you slipped." *African - Proverb*

"When you make a mistake, admit it. If you don't, you only make matters worse."

- Ward Cleaver, "Leave It To Beaver"

"Mistakes are the portals of discovery."

- James Joyce

"Every great mistake has a halfway moment, a split second when it can be recalled and perhaps remedied."

- Pearl S. Buck

Mistakes

Let a mistake occur, and the stream of remarks starts flowing: "We failed. They'll blame it on me. It's not my fault. There must be a traitor someplace. Once again, I screwed up. I can't seem to do anything right. Just my luck to get saddled with a bunch of idiots who don't know what they're doing. Does anyone know how to do this the right way? Hasn't anybody ever taught them?"

Sadly, there are elements of truth in explosive remarks. The bigger question is how people's mindsets toward mistakes and failures got that way. Things we do that set us up for failure include:

- Remembering things like they once were...trying to recreate as we believe they were.
- Doing things purely for creative fulfillment...without comprehending the realities.
- Thinking that business acquaintances really care about us as human beings.
- Expecting that others will treat us as fairly as we treat them.
- Hoping that volunteer contributions to the community will be repaid in business referrals.

NEGOTIATIONS, COMPROMISE

"It takes two to tango."

- Proverb

"Never hold discussions with the monkey when the organ grinder is in the room."

- Sir Winston Churchill

"Let us never negotiate out of fear, but let us never fear to negotiate."

- President John F. Kennedy

"Force without wisdom falls of its own weight." Horace "Pure reason avoids extremes, and requires one to be wise in moderation."

- Moliere

"Anybody who accepts mediocrity - in school, on the job, in life - is a person who compromises, and when the leader compromises, the whole organization compromises."

- Charles Knight

"A compromise is the art of dividing a cake in such a way that everyone believes he has the biggest piece."

- Ludwig Erhard

"If you limit your choices only to what seems possible or reasonable, you disconnect yourself from what you truly want, and all that is left is a compromise."

- Robert Fritz

"Come, let us reason together."

- President Lyndon B. Johnson

"Discourage litigation. Persuade your neighbors to compromise whenever you can. As a peacemaker the lawyer has superior opportunity of being a good man. There will still be business enough."

- President Abraham Lincoln

"Peace won by the compromise of principles is a short-lived achievement."

- Anonymous

Negotiations, Compromise

Research tells us that all of us agree on 95% of things. It's that 5% where we disagree that gets us into unnecessary confrontations. Too many organizations choose the wrong causes to fight...thus defeating the shared goals, opportunities and marketplace advantages which they may have had.

Business needs to pursue negotiations before resorting to litigation. Similarly, drawing one's line in the sand tends to negate future opportunities for negotiations and compromise.

OPPORTUNITY

"Opportunity can often sway even an honest man."
- Latin proverb

"A wise man will make more opportunities than he finds."
- Sir Francis Bacon

"All's grist that comes to the mill. Every dog has his day.
Hoist your sail when the wind is fair. Make hay while the sun shines. Nothing ventured, nothing gained. Opportunity seldom knocks twice. Strike while the iron is hot."
- Proverbs

"He who sees the last blossom on the plum tree must pick it."
- Chinese proverb

"Opportunities are usually disguised as hard work, so most people don't recognize them."
- Ann Landers

"There is no security in this life. There is only opportunity."
- General Douglas MacArthur

"Equality of opportunity means equal opportunity to be unequal."
- Iain Macleod

"Grab a chance and you won't be sorry for a might have been."
- Arthur Ransome

"Never miss a chance to have sex or appear on television."
- Gore Vidal

"I know not, sir, whether Bacon wrote the works of Shakespeare, but if he did not it seems to me that he missed the opportunity of his life."
- James Barrie

"Opportunity is missed by most people because it is dressed in overalls and looks like work."
- Thomas Edison

"Always acknowledge a fault. This will throw those in authority off their guard and give you an opportunity to commit more."
- Mark Twain

"Equal opportunity means everyone will have a fair chance at being incompetent."
- Laurence J. Peter

"An empowered organization is one in which individuals have the knowledge, skill, desire and opportunity to succeed in a way that leads to collective organizational success."
- Stephen Covey

"Men make history, and not the other way around. In periods where there is no leadership, society stands still. Progress occurs when courageous, skillful leaders seize the opportunity to change things for the better."

- President Harry S. Truman

"You have to recognize when the right place and time and take advantage of that opportunity. There are plenty of opportunities out there. You can't sit back and wait."

- Ellen Metcalf

"Seize opportunity by the beard, for it is bald behind."

- Bulgarian Proverb

"The Chinese use two brush strokes to write the word 'crisis.' One brush stroke stands for danger; the other for opportunity. In a crisis, be aware of the danger, but recognize the opportunity."

- Richard M. Nixon

"A pessimist sees the difficulty in every opportunity; an optimist sees the opportunity in every difficulty."

- Sir Winston Churchill

"In the middle of difficulty lies opportunity. Never regard study as a duty, but as the enviable opportunity to learn to know the liberating influence of beauty in the realm of the spirit for your own joy and to the profit of the community to which your later work belongs."

- Albert Einstein

"Opportunity may knock only once, but temptation leans on the doorbell. Many an opportunity is lost because a man is out looking for four-leaf clovers."

- Anonymous

"Time goes by so fast, people go in and out of your life. You must never miss the opportunity to tell these people how much they mean to you."

- "Cheers" TV series

"It is better to be prepared for an opportunity and not have one

than to have an opportunity and not be prepared."
- Whitney Young, Jr.

"Ability is of little account without opportunity."
- Napoleon Bonaparte

"Luck is what happens when preparation meets opportunity."
- Seneca

"He who refuses to embrace a unique opportunity loses the prize as surely as if he had failed."
- William James

"I believe that every right implies a responsibility; every opportunity an obligation; every possession a duty."
- John D. Rockefeller, Jr.

"If someone says "can't," that shows you what to do."
- John Cage

"Problems are only opportunities in work clothes."
- Henry J. Kaiser

"Breaks balance out. The sun don't shine on the same ol' dog's ass every day."
- Darrell Royal

"Life is a series of inspired follies. The difficulty is to find them to do. Never lose a chance: it doesn't come every day."
- George Bernard Shaw

"I am open to receive With every breath I breathe."
- Michael Sun

"The sun! The sun! And all we can become!"
- Theodore Roethke

"We are wide-eyed in contemplating the possibility that life may exist elsewhere in the universe, but we wear blinders

when contemplating the possibilities of life on earth."
- Norman Cousins

"A wise man will make more opportunities than he finds."
- Sir Francis Bacon

"A pessimist is one who makes difficulties of his opportunities; an optimist is one who makes opportunities of his difficulties."
- Reginald B. Mansell

"The opportunity that God sends does not wake up him who is asleep."
- Senegalese Proverb

"Many are called, but few get up."
- Oliver Herford

"Many do with opportunities as children do at the seashore, they fill their little hands with sand, and then let the grains fall through, one by one, till all are gone."
- Thomas Jones

"Observe the opportunity."
- Ecclesiasticus

"There are joys which long to be ours. God sends ten thousand truths, which come about us like birds seeking inlet; but we are shut up to them, and so they bring us nothing, but sit and sing awhile upon the roof, and then fly away."
- Henry Ward Beecher

"When life gives you oranges, enjoy. When life gives you lemons, make lemonade."
- Anonymous

"There's so much speculating going on that a lot of us never get around to living. Life is always walking up to us and saying, "Come on in, the living's fine," and what do we do? Back off and take its picture."

- Russell Baker

"Learn to listen. Opportunity could be knocking at your door very softly."

- Frank Tyger

"Problems are a chance for you to do your best."

- Duke Ellington

"Never regard study as a duty, but as the enviable opportunity to learn to know the liberating influence of beauty in the realm of the spirit for your own personal joy and to the profit of the community to which your later work belongs."

- Albert Einstein

"Watch out for emergencies. They are your big chance!"

- Fritz Reiner

CHAPTER 9

Perspectives on Life...Perceptions and Realities
Philanthropy, Charity, Community Involvement
Philosophy
Planning
Power
Pride

PERSPECTIVES ON LIFE...
PERCEPTIONS AND REALITIES

"All that we see or seem is but a dream within a dream."
- *Edgar Allan Poe*

"Cross the street with your eyes."
- *Howdy Doody*

"I saw it, but I did not realize it."
- *Elizabeth Peabody*

"If the doors of perception were cleansed, everything would appear to man as it is, infinite. Man's desires are limited by his perceptions. None can desire what he has not perceived."
- *William Blake*

"Hey life, look at me. I can see through reality. Now I see life for what it is. It's not a dream. It's not a bliss. It happened to me, and it can happen to you."
- "The Happening," *Diana Ross & the Supremes*

"When you cease to make a contribution, you begin to die."
- *Eleanor Roosevelt*

"Humankind cannot bear much reality. Between the idea and the reality, between the motion and the act, falls the shadow."
- *T.S. Eliot*

"I've looked at life from both sides now. Those bright illusions I recall. I really don't know life at all."
- *Judy Collins*

"Farming looks mighty easy when your plow is a pencil and you're a thousand miles from a cornfield."
- *President Dwight D. Eisenhower* (1956)

"The superior man is satisfied and composed. The mean man is always full of distress. The superior man is distressed by his want of ability. When you meet someone better than yourself, turn your thoughts to becoming his equal. When you meet someone not as good as you are, look within and examine your own self."

- Confucius

"I am not a pessimist; to perceive evil where it exists is, in my opinion, a form of optimism."

- Roberto Rossellini

"Optimism is a mania for maintaining that all is well when things are going badly."

- Voltaire

"An optimist may see a light where there is none, but why must the pessimist always run to blow it out?"

- Michel de Saint-Pierre

"It is the commonest of mistakes to consider that the limit of our power of perception is also the limit of all there is to perceive."

- C. W. Leadbeater

"Have no fear of perfection...you'll never reach it."

- Salvador Dali

"Nothing would be done at all if a man waited until he could do it so well that no one could find fault with it."

- Cardinal Newman

"Never give in. Never. Never. Never. Never."

- Sir Winston Churchill

"Keep walking and keep smiling."

- Tiny Tim

"Fall seven times, stand up eight."

- Japanese Proverb

"Nothing I do can't be done by a 10-year-old with 15 years of practice."

- Harry Blackstone Jr.

"Pick yourself up, dust yourself off, start all over again."

- Dorothy Fields

"I will neither yield to the song of the siren nor the voice of the hyena, the tears of the crocodile nor the howling of the wolf."

- George Chapman

"Victory belongs to the most persevering."

- Napoleon Bonaparte

"To dry one's eyes and laugh at a fall, And baffled, get up and begin again."

- Robert Browning

"By perseverance the snail reached the ark."

- Charles Haddon Spurgeon

"Perseverance is more prevailing than violence; and many things which cannot be overcome when they are together, yield themselves up when taken little by little."

'- Plutarch

"You do not need to leave your room. Remain sitting at your table and listen. Do not even listen, simply wait. Do not even wait, be quite still and solitary. The world will freely offer itself to you to be unmasked, it has no choice, it will roll in ecstasy at your feet."

- Franz Kafka

"To be conscious that we are perceiving or thinking is to be conscious of our own existence."

- Aristotle

"I am a camera with its shutter open, passive, recording, not thinking. Recording the man shaving at the window opposite and the woman in the kimono washing her hair."
- *Christopher Isherwood*

"To become the spectator of one's own life is to escape the suffering of life."
- *Oscar Wilde*

PHILANTHROPY, CHARITY, COMMUNITY INVOLVEMENT

Every organization has an obligation to give back to the communities in which it does business. That includes non-profit organizations and public sector agencies that in turn ask the private sector for support, advice and in-kind donations.

Certainly, companies are not there to give everything back. They are in business to make good products-services, earn fair returns on investment and reward employees for jobs well done. A portion of that investment lies in the communities in which we live, work and thrive.

Corporate contributions should be budgeted and may be thought of as a part of business development, public relations and marketing. It is advantageous to make donations according to a philanthropy plan that is conducive to the corporate culture, goals and core values. One cannot support all causes for all reasons. By defining fields of interest and spreading the resources around fairly, the company can support more causes and amass more goodwill.

Banking goodwill in the community helps the company when it needs to call upon local resources. It underscores the company's empowerment of employees. Companies with employee guilds-clubs tend to show three times the amount of worker loyalty and productivity.

Executives of the companies have an obligation to be seen as community leaders. This process widens their leadership skills, which can be reapplied back at the company. Younger employees must be taught that community participation is a part of their job and is essential to their executive grooming.

Some of the best deals are cut because of relationships cemented at board meetings and philanthropy events. Many companies utilize their public personas to engage support of collaborators, vendors and other business partners.

Giving back to the community is good for business...and it is the right thing to do. This continuum results from earnestly supporting public causes and activities, without hidden agendas. Business is and should be about doing the right things for the right reasons. Thereafter, everyone benefits from community goodwill.

PHILOSOPHY

"I have had a dream, past the wit of man to say what dream it was. We are such stuff as dreams are made on, and our little life is rounded with a sleep."

- William Shakespeare

"Once Chuang Chou dreamt he was a butterfly, flitting and fluttering around, happy with himself and doing as he pleased. He didn't know he was Chuang Chou. Suddenly he woke up and there he was, solid and unmistakeable Chuang Chou. But he didn't know if he was Chuang Chou who had dreamt he was a butterfly, or a butterfly dreaming he was Chuang Chou."

- Chaung Tzu

"We are the miracle of force and matter making itself over into imagination and will. Incredible. The Life Force experimenting with forms. You for one. Me for another. The Universe has shouted itself alive. We are one of the shouts."

- Ray Bradbury

"Mind is locked in matter like the spirit Ariel in a cloven pine. Men struggle to escape the drag of the matter they inhabit, yet it is the spirit they fear. You think that way as you begin to get grayer and you see pretty plainly that the game is not going to end as you planned. Content is a word unknown to life; it is also a word unknown to man."

- Loren Eiseley

"A moment's halt - a momentary taste of being from the well amid the waste. And lo, the phantom caravan has reached the nothing it set out from - oh, make haste!"

- Omar Khayyam

"Yield to temptation. It may not pass your way again."

- Robert Heinlein

"The reasonable man adapts himself to the world. The unreasonable one persists in trying to adapt the world to himself. Progress depends on the unreasonable man."

- George Bernard Shaw

"If the doors of perception were cleansed, every thing would appear to man as it is, infinite."

- William Blake

"I wake to sleep, and take my waking slow. I feel my fate in what I cannot fear. I learn by going where I have to go."

Theodore Roethke

"I see my life go drifting like a river from change to change. I have been many things: a green drop in the surge, a gleam of light upon a sword, a fir tree on a hill, an old slave grinding a heavy quern, a king sitting upon a chair of gold. Now I have grown nothing, knowing all."

- William Butler Yeats

"There comes a time in each life like a point of fulcrum. At that time you must accept yourself. It is not any more what you will become. It is what you are and always will be. The most important questions in life can never be answered by anyone except oneself."

- John Fowles

"Only that day dawns to which we are awake. There is more day to dawn. The sun is but a morning star."

- Henry David Thoreau, "Walden"

"What is important in life is life, and not the result of life. One lives but once in the world. Art is long, life short; judgment difficult, opportunity transient. Time does not relinquish its rights, either over human beings or over mountains. Man errs as long as he strives. I love those who yearn for the impossible."

- Johann Wolfgang von Goethe

"We dance round in a ring and suppose, but the Secret sits in the middle and knows."

- Robert Frost

"We feel that even if all possible scientific questions be answered, the problems of life have still not been touched at all. Of course, there is then no question left, and just this is the answer. The solution of the problem of life is seen in the vanishing of this problem."

- Ludwig Wittgenstein

"We shall not cease from exploration. And the end of all our exploring will be to arrive where we started and know the place for the first time."

- T. S. Eliot

"If you stop searching, you stop living, because then you're dwelling in the past. If you're not reaching forward to any growth or future, you might as well be dead."

- Wynn Bullock

"That is what learning is. You suddenly understand something you've understood all your life, but in a new way."
- Doris Lessing, The Four-Gated City

Philosophy

Core values form the basis for motivations to succeed in business. Vision is the stream of realities, processes, planning and measurements by which long-term successes care amassed. Philosophies are developed along the road of hard knocks. They transition our dreams into practicabilities. They measure our successes and failures and give us the perspectives to persevere.

These are some of the philosophies that I have developed about business and its relationships to life, communities, stakeholders and its reasons for being:

The potentiality of organizations is a progressive journey from information to insight. As I said in the introduction, foolhardiness is being righteous about things at the wrong times. People and organizations spend disproportionate amounts of time trying to be or look like someone else...or what they think others look like. Until one becomes one's own best, the futile trail continues.

It takes more courage to pursue a compromise than to pursue an extremist position. Conciliation and reason must be pursued. The skill with which they are approached often spells the difference between total success and political suicide.

People spend so much time relating to and craving the past... or what they think it was. They go to great lengths to recreate the past and devote their lives to avoiding and fighting change.

People take inordinate risks to pursue forbidden things. But what risks will they take to pursue the truth? People believe lies and gossip faster than they believe the truth.

Individuals and organizations have changed and adapted more than they think. Standing still means moving backward. If they would move forward with their lives, the past would reflect new knowledge. Today is more vivid in people's minds than the past. Today reflects past changes. Tomorrow represents the opportunity to live the kind of life that you want, be the person you have been preparing to be, and become the kind of organization that is successful, rather than dwelling upon past failures and shortcomings.

Take what you don't want to believe. Add what you have to believe. You come up with amazing answers. Expect the best, but prepare for the worst. There is no plan that is foolproof. Fight for and with the truth. Truth is not always easy to recognize and not always pretty.

There is no such thing as perfection. Continuous quality improvement means that we benchmark accomplishments and set the next reach a little further.

Things are never simple for one who must make decisions and policies. Many factors must be weighed. There are contexts and subtle nuances to most business decisions. One cannot always go the path that seems clearest. One who thinks differently and creatively will face opposition. With success of the concept, it gets embraced by others, who claim to have been visionary all along. Shepherding good ideas and concepts does not get many external plaudits. The feeling of accomplishment must be internal. That is a true mark of wisdom.

A great mentor, teacher and role model need not be from the same strata as those whom he-she inspires. Top executives must set standards that others aspire to...including themselves.

People and companies which prefer substance exhibit it by exceeding all standards. Set and meet realistic benchmarks for success. Approach change as an opportunity. Continue asking for feedback. Regularly update policies and procedures. Employ a "futurist" mentality.

PLANNING

"The beginning is the most important part of the work."
- Plato

"A good plan violently executed now is better than a perfect plan next week."
- General George S. Patton

"If I had known my son was going to be president of Bolivia, I would have taught him to read and write."
- Enrique Penaranda's mother

"You've got to be very careful if you don't know where you are going, because you might not get there."
- Yogi Berra

"I always wanted to be somebody, but I should have been more specific."
- Lily Tomlin

"When we are planning for posterity, we ought to remember that virtue is not hereditary."
- Thomas Paine

"The best victory is when the opponent surrenders of its own accord before there are any actual hostilities. It is best to win without fighting."
- Sun-tzu, "The Art of War"

"Good plans shape good decisions. That's why good planning helps to make elusive dreams come true."
- Lester R. Bittel, "The Nine Master Keys of Management"

"If anything is certain, it is that change is certain. The world we are planning for today will not exist in this form tomorrow."
- Philip Crosby, "Reflections on Quality"

"What business strategy is all about; what distinguishes it from all other kinds of business planning is, in a word, competitive advantage. Without competitors there would be no need for strategy, for the sole purpose of strategic planning is to enable the company to gain, as effectively as possible, a sustainable edge over its competitors."

- Keniche Ohnae

"Men often oppose a thing merely because they have had no agency in planning it, or because it may have been planned by those whom they dislike."

- Alexander Hamilton

"In preparing for battle I have always found that plans are useless, but planning is indispensable."

- President Dwight D. Eisenhower

Planning

Getting the funds that you need from tight fisted management is an ongoing process. Cash outlays are justifiable either by dollars they bring in or dollars they stand to save for the organization. Cash outlays are always risks. Justify your risks in proportion to riskier ones they have previously funded. Validate your worth to the overall company operation. Under the rules of supply chain dynamics, one must study your supplier relationships, formalize a plan of outsourcing and develop collaborations.

In requesting additional funds, take money with you. Show returns or savings on previous appropriations. Position your request as an investment, not a cost. Sell management-clients on acquiring more returns on their investments, not just on making further investments.

To advance your funding process, be visible when funds are flowing. Reduce management's risk in doing business with you. Be a consistent producer of profit-improving outcomes, not just a spotty or hit-and-miss producer. Put money in management's pockets. Get to the front of the line for funding requests. Acquire an upper-management mindset. Condense the funding cycle. Become top management's partner in efficiency of operations.

POWER

"Power corrupts, but lack of power corrupts absolutely."
- Adlai Stevenson

"Power corrupts the few, while weakness corrupts the many. Absolute faith corrupts as absolutely as absolute power."
- Eric Hoffer

"Whenever there's a large group of powers, they always follow the one with the biggest bomb."
- John F. Kennedy

"Power does not corrupt. Fear corrupts, perhaps the fear of a loss of power."
- John Steinbeck

"Nearly all men can stand adversity, but if you want to test a man's character, give him power."
- President Abraham Lincoln

"Power does not corrupt men. But fools, if they get into a position of power, corrupt it. The power of accurate observation is commonly called cynicism by those who have not got it."
- George Bernard Shaw

"Our scientific power has outrun our spiritual power. We have guided missiles and misguided men."

- Martin Luther King Jr.

"If computers get too powerful, we can organize them into a committee. That will do them in."

- Bradley's Bromide

"A cult is a religion with no political power."

- Tom Wolfe

"If mankind minus one were of one opinion, then mankind is no more justified in silencing the one than the one, if he had the power, would be justified in silencing mankind."

- John Stuart Mill

"There is danger from all men. The only maxim of a free government ought to be to trust no man living with power to endanger the public liberty."

- John Adams

"The greatest mystery is not that we have been flung at random between the profusion of matter and of the stars, but that within this prison we can draw from ourselves images powerful enough to deny our nothingness."

- Andre Malraux

"The power of hiding ourselves from one another is mercifully given, for men are wild beasts, and would devour one another but for this protection."

- Henry Ward Beecher, "Proverbs from Plymouth Pulpit"

PRIDE

"Pride is the never failing vice of fools."

- Alexander Pope

"Misquotation is, in fact, the pride and privilege of the learned. A widely-read man never quotes accurately, for the rather obvious reason that he has read too widely."

- Hesketh Pearson

"Eccentricity is not, as dull people would have us believe, a form of madness. It is often a kind of innocent pride, and the man of genius and the aristocrat are frequently regarded as eccentrics because genius and aristocrat are entirely unafraid of and uninfluenced by the opinions and vagaries of the crowd."

- Edith Sitwell

"Be modest! It is the kind of pride least likely to offend."

- Jules Renard

"Generosity is giving more than you can, and pride is taking less than you need."

- Kahlil Gibran

"To find yourself jilted is a blow to your pride. Do your best to forget it and if you don't succeed, at least pretend to."

- Moliere

"Don't think of retiring from the world until the world will be sorry that you retire. I hate a fellow whom pride or cowardice or laziness drives into a corner, and who does nothing when he is there but sit and growl. Let him come out as I do, and bark."

- Samuel Johnson

CHAPTER 10

Reputation
Respect
Responsibility and Accountability
Results, Benchmarking, Measurements
Rigidity — Reluctance to Progress

REPUTATION

"Reputation is the jewel of one's soul."

- William Shakespeare

"Associate yourself with men of good quality if you esteem your own reputation for 'tis better to be alone than in bad company."
- George Washington

"Ninety percent of the politicians give the other ten percent a bad reputation."

- Henry Kissinger

"It pays to be obvious, especially if you have a reputation for subtlety."

- Isaac Asimov

"Until you've lost your reputation, you never realize what a burden it was."

- Margaret Mitchell

"One can survive everything, nowadays, except death, and live down everything except a good reputation."

- Oscar Wilde

"Few people think more than two or three times a year; I have made an international reputation for myself by thinking once or twice a week."

- George Bernard Shaw

"You can't build a reputation on what you are going to do."
- Henry Ford

"Self-esteem is the reputation we acquire with ourselves."
- Nathaniel Branden

"A good reputation is more valuable than money."
- Publilius Syrus

"There are people who strictly deprive themselves of each and every eatable, drinkable, and smokable which has in any way acquired a shady reputation. They pay this price for health. And health is all they get for it. How strange it is. It is like paying out your whole fortune for a cow that has gone dry."

- Mark Twain

"Conscience and reputation are two things. Conscience is due to yourself, reputation to your neighbor."

- Saint Augustine

"Property left to a child may soon be lost;. A good name and unblemished reputation will abide forever. If those who are toiling for wealth to leave their children, would but take half the pains to secure for them virtuous habits, how much more serviceable would they be. The largest property may be wrested from a child, but virtue will stand by him to the last."

- William Graham Sumner

"There are two modes of establishing our reputation: to be praised by honest men, and to be abused by rogues. It is best, however, to secure the former, because it will invariably be accompanied by the latter."

- Charles Caleb Colton

"Propriety was a rigid master, but one that must be obeyed if one wanted to keep a sterling reputation."

- Lawana Blackwell, "The Courtship of the Vicar's Daughter"

"Reputation is what other people know about you. Honor is what you know about yourself. Guard your honor. Let your reputation fall where it will. And outlive the bastards."

- Lois McMaster Bujold, "A Civil Campaign"

"Regard your good name as the richest jewel you can possibly be possessed of...for credit is like fire; when once you have kindled it you may easily preserve it, but if you once extinguish it, you will find it an arduous task to rekindle it again. The way to gain a good reputation is to endeavor to be what you desire to appear."

- Socrates

Reputation

The professional organization that evokes a caring image and backs it up with service will prosper in today's marketplace. When image building, the following ideas should be considered:
- Your company and profession fill essential needs of society.
- Each key staff member represents a learned profession.
- Qualities that denote your company include skill, expertise, objectivity and independence.
- Work and abilities of your employees are diverse and creative.
- Your key management team is dynamic, in terms of business issues.
- The marketplace is rapidly expanding and is an excellent career choice for young people.
- Your team encompasses multi-dimensional professionals...concerned with much more than the immediate responsibilities of the work at hand.
- Recognize the role of professional communicators.
- Seek qualified counsel.

RESPECT

"Respect a man, he will do the more."

- James Howell

"If we paid more respect to the living than to the dead, then the world would be a better place."

- Sigmund Freud

"That you may retain your self-respect, it is better to displease

the people by doing what you know is right, than to temporarily please them by doing what you know is wrong."
- William J. H. Boetcker

"If you want to be respected, you must respect yourself."
- Spanish Proverb

"What you want, baby, I got. What you need, you know I got it. All I askin' is for a little respect. Find out what it means to me."
- Aretha Franklin

"We confide in our strength, without boasting of it; we respect that of others, without fearing it."
- President Thomas Jefferson

"He that respects himself is safe from others. He wears a coat of mail that none can pierce."
- Henry Wadsworth Longfellow

"In real life, unlike in Shakespeare, the sweetness of the rose depends upon the name it bears. Things are not only what they are. They are, in very important respects, what they seem to be."
- Vice President Hubert H. Humphrey

"I respect faith, but doubt is what gets you an education."
- Wilson Mizner

"The English have no respect for their language, and will not teach their children to speak it. The more things a man is ashamed of, the more respectable he is."
- George Bernard Shaw

"Some people have so much respect for their superiors they have none left for themselves."
- Peter McArthur

"To get back my youth I would do anything in the world, except

take exercise, get up early, or be respectable."
                                    - *Oscar Wilde*, "The Picture of Dorian Gray"

"I can win an argument on any topic, against any opponent. People know this, and steer clear of me at parties. Often, as a sign of their great respect, they don't even invite me."
                                    - *Dave Barry*

"One should as a rule respect public opinion in so far as is necessary to avoid starvation and to keep out of prison. Anything that goes beyond this is voluntary submission to an unnecessary tyranny, and is likely to interfere with happiness in all kinds of ways."
                                    - *Bertrand Russell*

"Consult your friend on all things, especially on those which respect yourself. His counsel may then be useful where your own self-love might impair your judgment."
                                    - *Seneca*

"Self-respect is the fruit of discipline; the sense of dignity grows with the ability to say no to oneself."
                                    - *Rabbi Abraham Heschel*

"Be peaceful, be courteous, obey the law, respect everyone; but if someone puts his hand on you, send him to the cemetery."
                                    - *Malcolm X*

"Never esteem anything as of advantage to you that will make you break your word or lose your self-respect."
                                    - *Marcus Aurelius Antoninus*

"I am a Conservative to preserve all that is good in our constitution, a Radical to remove all that is bad. I seek to preserve property and to respect order. I equally decry the appeal to the passions of the many of the prejudices of the few."
                                    - *Benjamin Disraeli*

"Character - the willingness to accept responsibility for one's own life - is the source from which self respect springs."
- Joan Didion, "Slouching Towards Bethlehem"

"I owe my success to having listened respectfully to the very best advice, and then going away and doing the exact opposite."
- G. K. Chesterton

"Self-respect is the cornerstone of all virtue."
- John Herschel

"Adulthood isn't an award they'll give you for being a good child. You can waste years, trying to get someone to give that respect to you, as though it were a sort of promotion or raise in pay. If only you do enough, if only you are good enough. No. You have to just take it. Give it to yourself, I suppose. Say, I'm sorry you feel like that and walk away. But that's hard."
- Lois McMaster Bujold, "A Civil Campaign"

"In your clothes, avoid too much gaudiness; do not value yourself upon an embroidered gown; and remember that a reasonable word, or an obliging look, will gain you more respect than all your fine trappings."
- Sir George Savile, "Advice to a Daughter"

Respect

The basics of good business are rooted in respect.

Respect is a valuable commodity that caring professionals must nurture and show toward their colleagues, customers, industry, marketplace and stakeholders.

These are the characteristics of good corporate strategies and, thus, company philosophies:
- Focus upon the customer.

- Honors the employees.
- Shows business life as a process, not a quick fix.
- Portrays their company as a contributor, not a savior.
- Clearly defines their niche.
- Says and does things that inspire you to think.
- Is compatible with other communications.
- Remains consistent with their products, services and track record.

These are the seven key traits of a successful company visioning program:

1. Effective visions are inspiring. They must touch the chords of what the company started out to become. They may compel leaders to renew or multiply their commitments for the future. Their messages can apply to every sector of the company.

2. Effective visions are clear and challenging...involving excellence. There is no such thing as perfection, but incremental levels of excellence are to be attained and bested. Every message must be communicated throughout the organization, acquiring feedback and additional commitments from the rank and file. Thereafter, visions become their brainchildren.

3. Effective visions have marketplace purpose, savvy and flexibility. It is not enough to look good on paper or touch the hearts of some. Visions must squarely place the company in the forefront of its market niche, customer base, industry perspective and economic realm. It's all about doing good business and then being a good organization.

4. Effective visions must be stable, yet prudently updated. No "pie in the sky" tenets or trite restatements of other companies' promotions are acceptable. Show how planned, controlled growth will maintain stability for investors, hold interest for the marketplace and propel the organization to break further new ground.

5. Effective visions are role models, when all else is in turmoil.

Research shows that only 2% of the world's companies have strategic plans. Visioning programs go far beyond the plan and root the corporate culture into something real and breathing. While most companies meander, your visionary company can chart its own course.

6. Effective visions empower the organization's people first and the customers secondly. People constitute the largest component (28%) of a successful organization. They are neglected because they are not consulted or considered. By nurturing the company's best resource (its people), then productivity, creativity and profitability soar. At all times, what is done and accomplished must focus upon the customer base.

7. Effective visions honor the past and prepare for the future. There are good reasons why the company started. By weathering change and taking new turns, the organization matures. With futures constantly changing, then the art of success comes from re-examining the journey. From the subtlest nuances come gems of gold in the organization's bank.

RESPONSIBILITY AND ACCOUNTABILITY

"The buck stops here."
- President Harry S. Truman

"A bad workman always blames his tools."
- Proverb

"Each man the architect of his own fate."
- Appius Caecus

"You're either part of the solution or part of the problem."
- Eldridge Cleaver

"When your neighbor's wall is on fire, it becomes your business."

- Horace

"In dreams begins responsibility."

- W.B. Yeats

"There is no accountability in the public school system, except for coaches. You know what happens to a losing coach. You fire him. A losing teacher can go on losing for 30 years and then go to glory."

- Ross Perot

"We are at the very beginning of time for the human race. It is not unreasonable that we grapple with problems. But there are tens of thousands of years in the future. Our responsibility is to do what we can, learn what we can, improve the solutions, and pass them on."

- Richard Feynman

"The price of greatness is responsibility."

- Sir Winston Churchill

"So many new ideas are at first strange and horrible, though ultimately valuable that a very heavy responsibility rests upon those who would prevent their dissemination."

- John Haldane

"Forming characters! Whose? Our own or others? Both. And in that momentous fact lies the peril and responsibility of our existence."

- Elihu Burritt

"You cannot escape the responsibility of tomorrow by evading it today."

- Abraham Lincoln

"Character - the willingness to accept responsibility for one's

own life - is the source from which self respect springs."
- *Joan Didion*, "Slouching Towards Bethlehem"

"I think of a hero as someone who understands the degree of responsibility that comes with his freedom."
- *Bob Dylan*

"The more freedom we enjoy, the greater the responsibility we bear, toward others as well as ourselves."
- *Oscar Arias Sanchez*

"Liberty means responsibility. That is why most men dread it."
- *George Bernard Shaw*

"The fault, dear Brutus, is not in our stars but in ourselves. No one familiar with the history of this country can deny that Congressional committees are useful. It is necessary to investigate before legislating. But the line between investigating and persecuting is a fine one. And the junior senator from Wisconsin has stepped over it repeatedly. We must remember that accusation is not proof and that conviction depends on evidence and due process of law.

We will not walk in fear of one another. We will not be driven by fear into an age of unreason. If we dig deeply in our history and doctrines, we remember we are not descended from fearful men...not from men who feared to write, to speak, to associate with and to defend causes which were for the moment unpopular. This is no time for men who oppose Senator McCarthy's methods to keep silent.

We can deny our heritage and our history. But we cannot evade responsibility for the result of it. There is no way for a citizen of a republic to abdicate these responsibilities. We proclaim ourselves—as indeed we are—the defenders of freedom, what's left of it. But we cannot defend freedom abroad by deserting it at home. The actions of the junior senator from Wisconsin have caused alarm and dismay amongst our allies abroad, and given considerable comfort to our enemies.

And whose fault is that? Not really his. He didn't create this situation of fear. He merely exploited it...and rather successfully.

Cassius was right. The fault, dear Brutus, is not in our stars but in ourselves."

- Edward R. Murrow

Responsibility and Accountability

Integrity is personal and professional. It is about more than the contents of a financial report. It bespeaks to every aspect of the way in which we do business. Integrity requires consistency and the enlightened self-interest of doing a better job.

Financial statements by themselves cannot nor ever were intended to determine company value. The enlightened company must be structured, plan and benchmark according to all seven categories on my trademarked Business Tree™: core business, running the business, financial, people, business development, Body of Knowledge (interaction of each part to the other and to the whole) and The Big Picture (who the organization really is, where it is going and how it will successfully get there).

One need not fear business nor think ill of it because of the recent corporate scandals. One need not fear globalization and expansion of business because of economic recessions. It is during the downturns that strong, committed and ethical businesses renew their energies to move forward. The good apples polish their luster in such ways as to distance from the few bad apples.

Corporate Responsibility means operating a business in ways that meet or exceed the ethical, legal, commercial and public expectations that society has of business. This is a comprehensive set of strategies, methodologies, policies, practices and programs that are integrated throughout business operations, supported and rewarded by top management.

The growth of corporate responsibility as an issue and a

mandate in the New Order of Business stems from several events and trends:

- Changing expectations of stakeholders regarding business.
- Government's reduced role in a deregulated era.
- Increased customer interest and pressure.
- Supply chain responsibility in the age of collaborations, outsourcing and partnering.
- Growing investor insistence upon accountability.
- Intensively competitive labor markets.
- Voiced concerns by activist organizations.
- Demands for increased communication and disclosure.
- Emerging issues that widen the scope of business.
- Identification of new pockets of stakeholders.

The value of corporate responsibility can be measured in quantitative and qualitative ways. Companies have experienced bottom-line benefits, including improved financial performance, reduced operating costs, access to capital, increased sales and customer loyalty, positive reactions to brand image and reputation, heightened productivity, employee commitments to quality, empowered loyal workforces and reduced regulatory oversight.

RESULTS, BENCHMARKING, MEASUREMENTS

"Desperate cuts must have desperate cures."

- Proverb

"You can do anything in this world if you are prepared to take the consequences."

- W. Somerset Maugham

"The reward of a thing well done is to have done it."
- Ralph Waldo Emerson

"In nature, there are neither rewards nor punishments. There are consequences."
- Robert G. Ingersoll

"War is a series of catastrophes that results in a victory."
- Georges Clemenceau

"Don't tell people how to do things. Tell them what to do and let them surprise you with their results."
- General George S. Patton

"Insanity is doing the same thing over and over again and expecting different results."
- Albert Einstein

"Medicine is a collection of uncertain prescriptions the results of which, taken collectively, are more fatal than useful to mankind."
- Napoleon Bonaparte

"Dreams surely are difficult, confusing, and not everything in them is brought to pass for mankind. For fleeting dreams have two gates: one is fashioned of horn and one of ivory. Those which pass through the one of sawn ivory are deceptive, bringing tidings which come to nought, but those which issue from the one of polished horn bring true results when a mortal sees them."
- Homer, "The Odyssey"

"For the truth of the conclusions of physical science, observation is the supreme Court of Appeal. It does not follow that every item which we confidently accept as physical knowledge has actually been certified by the Court.

Our confidence is that it would be certified by the Court if it were submitted. But it does follow that every item of physical knowledge is of a form which might be submitted to the

Court. It must be such that we can specify (although it may be impracticable to carry out) an observational procedure which would decide whether it is true or not.

Clearly a statement cannot be tested by observation unless it is an assertion about the results of observation. Every item of physical knowledge must therefore be an assertion of what has been or would be the result of carrying out a specified observational procedure."

- Sir Arthur Eddington, The Philosophy of Physical Science

"Advice is judged by results, not by intentions."

- Cicero

"You ask me why I do not write something. I think one's feelings waste themselves in words. They ought all to be distilled into actions and into actions which bring results."

- Florence Nightingale

"Results! Why, man, I have gotten a lot of results. I know several thousand things that won't work."

- Thomas A. Edison

Results, Benchmarking, Measurements

Fundamental to strategic planning is that the goals and objectives be tied to measurable activities. Gaining confidence is crucial, as business relationships are established to be long-term in duration. Each organization or should determine and craft its own character and personality...seeking to differentiate from others.

Effective benchmarks must be applied to all aspects of the business: Core Business, Running the Business, Financial, People and the interrelationship of these five major business functions to each other.

Benchmarking usually shows that customer service suffers during fast-growth periods. They have to back-pedal and recover customer confidence by doing surveys. Even with results of deteriorating customer service, growth-track companies pay lip service to really fixing their own problems.

Public perceptions are called "credence goods" by economists. Every organization must educate outside publics about what they do and how they do it. This premise also holds true for each corporate operating unit and department. The whole of the business and each subset must always educate corporate opinion makers on how it functions and the skill with which the company operates. Top management must endorse corporate communications, if your company is to grow and prosper.

Benchmarking for success is a factor of how diverse the company can and would like to be. Diversity is an enlightened mindset that affects workforce dynamics, plateaus of professionalism, work ethics, jobs and careers. Diversity embodies what it takes to succeed long-term, by diversifying the product mix, marketplace and customer focus. Every company is affected by external influences, and a diversity of ideas directly leads to pro-active approaches and measurements of achievements. Diversity is about the organization being all they can be, attaining levels of standards and questing for more. The wider scope that one takes with diversity, then it will be more embraced and coveted.

Business Model is a term that some people use to criticize the business failures of others. Few businesses are ever modeled. Business models relate to financial structures only, which represent less than 10% of the importance of each business. Less than two percent of businesses have strategic plans, which are umbrella frameworks for success. Business needs to strategize and plan first, with models for each sub-heading (core business, running the business, financial, people, business development, body of knowledge and the Big Picture) addressed.

To many people, the dotcom Bust was a crashing blow to business. Actually, it was a much-needed market correction, with liberal doses of reality. Too many dotcom companies were predicated upon fluff, hype and over-exaggeration. Owners felt they were exempt from the corporate practices and protocols of older companies. Analysts and those in the media who publicized companies' spins without investigating their facts were partly to blame. So-called "new school" ideologies proved to be tech excuses for not planning and developing corporate visions. Worthwhile fledgling companies now have greater chances of success in the future because a brief time of worshipping companies with no products and processes was exposed. As business moves forward, companies of substance will prosper.

Today's workforce needs three times the amount of training they are now getting in order to remain competitive and optimally productive. There is a difference between how one is basically educated and the ingredients needed to succeed in the long-term. Many people never amass those ingredients because they stop learning or don't see the need to go any further. Many people think they are "going further" but otherwise spin their wheels. There is a large disconnect between indoctrinating people to tools of the trade and the myriad of elements they will need to assimilate for their own futures. Training vendors sell what they have to provide...not what the constituencies or workforces need. Emphasis must be placed upon properly diagnosing the organization as a whole and then prescribing treatments for the whole, as well as the parts. Training should be conducted within a formal, planned program that addresses the majority of organizational aspects.

People who rise in upper corporate ranks do so for reasons other than themselves. The art is to understand and work with those factors, rather than to become a pawn of them. Executive development is a finely tuned art. It is a tireless yet energizing process. The old ways of rising to the top have changed. The savvy executive masters the new ways. Don't become a "flavor of the month." Trends and fads in business and in people will subside. Posture yourself for the long-run. Develop and trust your gut instinct. It's right most of the time.

RIGIDITY—RELUCTANCE TO PROGRESS

"A foolish consistency is the hobgoblin of little minds, adored by little statesmen and philosophers and divines."
- *Ralph Waldo Emerson*

"Only two things are infinite, the universe and human stupidity, and I'm not sure about the former."
- *Albert Einstein*

"Small things amuse small minds."
- *Doris Lessing*

"Obstinate people can be divided into the opinionated, the ignorant, and the boorish."
- *Aristotle*

"His mind is open. Yes, it is so open that nothing is retained. Ideas simply pass through him."
- *F.H. Bradley, British philosopher*

"Like all weak men, he laid an exaggerated stress on not changing one's mind."
- *W. Somerset Maugham*

"To resist the frigidity of old age one must combine the body, the mind and the heart - and to keep them in parallel vigor one must exercise, study and love."
- *Karl von Bonstetten*

"None so blind as those who won't see. You can lead a horse to the water, but you can't make him drink. Artificial Intelligence

is no match for natural stupidity. He that boasts of his own knowledge proclaims his ignorance. By ignorance is pride increased; those must assume who know the least."
- Proverbs

"I am firm; you are obstinate; he is a pig-headed fool."
- Bertrand Russell

"Genius may have its limitations, but stupidity is not thus handicapped."
- Elbert Hubbard

"Never attribute to malice what can be adequately explained by stupidity."
- Nick Diamos

"Egotism is the anesthetic that dulls the pain of stupidity."
- Frank Leahy

"To be stupid, selfish, and have good health are three requirements for happiness, though if stupidity is lacking, all is lost."
- Gustave Flaubert

"The two most common elements in the universe are Hydrogen and stupidity."
- Harlan Ellison

"With stupidity, the gods themselves contend in vain."
- Friedrich von Schiller

"You can never underestimate the stupidity of the general public."
- Scott Adams, "The Dilbert Future"

"At least two-thirds of our miseries spring from human stupidity, human malice and those great motivators and justifiers of malice and stupidity: idealism, dogmatism and proselytizing

zeal on behalf of religious or political ideas."
- Aldous Huxley

"Strange as it seems, no amount of learning can cure stupidity, and formal education positively fortifies it."
- Stephen Vizinczey

"Nothing in all the world is more dangerous than sincere ignorance and conscientious stupidity."
- Martin Luther King Jr., "Strength to Love"

"Books are hindrances to persisting stupidity."
- Spanish Proverb

"Tis sometimes the height of wisdom to feign stupidity."
- Cato the Elder

"Discourtesy does not spring merely from one bad quality, but from several—from foolish vanity, from ignorance of what is due to others, from indolence, from stupidity, from distraction of thought, from contempt of others, from jealousy."
- Jean de la Bruyere

"I don't even know what street Canada is on."
- Al Capone

"He who knows little often repeats it. He who knows nothing doubts nothing. What you don't know can't hurt you. Knowledge is the mother of virtue. Vice proceeds from ignorance."
- Proverbs

"Nothing in the world is more dangerous than sincere ignorance and conscientious stupidity."
- Martin Luther King, Jr.

"Ignorance is like a delicate exotic fruit. Touch it, and the bloom is gone."
- Oscar Wilde

"All you need in this life is ignorance and confidence, and then success is sure."

- Mark Twain

"Is sloppiness in speech caused by ignorance or apathy? I don't know and I don't care."

- William Safire

"One of the keys to happiness is a bad memory."

- Rita Mae Brown

"A person is never happy except at the price of some ignorance."

- Anatole France

"Education is a progressive discovery of our own ignorance."

- Will Durant

"A commercial and in some respects a social doubt has been started within the last year or two, whether or not it is right to discuss so openly the security or insecurity of locks. Many well-meaning persons suppose that the discussion respecting the means for baffling the supposed safety of locks offers a premium for dishonesty, by showing others how to be dishonest. This is a fallacy. Rogues are very keen in their profession, and already know much more than we can teach them respecting their several kinds of roguery. Rogues knew a good deal about lockpicking long before locksmiths discussed it among themselves, as they have lately done. If a lock — let it have been made in whatever country, or by whatever maker—is not so inviolable as it has hitherto been deemed to be, surely it is in the interest of "honest" persons to know this fact, because the "dishonest" are tolerably certain to be the first to apply the knowledge practically; and the spread of knowledge is necessary to give fair play to those who might suffer by ignorance. It cannot be too earnestly urged, that an acquaintance with real facts will, in the end, be better for all parties."

- Charles Tomlinson's Rudimentary Treatise on the
Construction of Locks

Hank Moore

"During almost 15 centuries, the legal establishment of Christianity has been upon trial. What has been its fruits? More or less, in all places, pride and indolence in the clergy; ignorance and servility in the laity; in both, superstition, bigotry, and persecution."

- President James Madison

"If today you can take a thing like evolution and make it a crime to teach in the public schools, tomorrow you can make it a crime to teach it in the private schools and next year you can make it a crime to teach it to the hustings or in the church. At the next session you may ban books and the newspapers... Ignorance and fanaticism are ever busy and need feeding. Always feeding and gloating for more. Today it is the public school teachers; tomorrow the private. The next day the preachers and the lecturers, the magazines, the books, the newspapers. After a while, Your Honor, it is the setting of man against man and creed against creed until with flying banners and beating drums we are marching backward to the glorious ages of the sixteenth centry when bigots lighted fagots to burn the men who dared to bring any intelligence and enlightenment and culture to the human mind."

- Clarence Darrow

"Ignorance is the soil in which belief in miracles grows."
- Robert G. Ingersoll

"Ignorance simplifies ANY problem."

- R. Lucke

"Its failings notwithstanding, there is much to be said in favor of journalism. By giving us the opinion of the uneducated, it keeps us in touch with the ignorance of the community."
- Oscar Wilde

"Let's not be too tough on our own ignorance. It's the thing that makes America great. If America weren't incomparably ignorant, how could we have tolerated the last eight years?"
- Frank Zappa

"Never ascribe to malice that which is caused by greed and ignorance."

- Cal Keegan

"It is better to be a beggar than ignorant; for a beggar only wants money, but an ignorant person wants humanity."

- Aristippus

"Ignorance, when voluntary, is criminal, and a man may be properly charged with that evil which he neglected or refused to learn how to prevent."

- Johnson

"Ignorance of all things is an evil neither terrible nor excessive, nor yet the greatest of all; but great cleverness and much learning, if they be accompanied by a bad training, are a much greater misfortune."

- Plato

Rigidity—Reluctance to Progress

Those who fight and thwart change will become victims of the inevitable shifts. Those who are not focused upon progress will feel run over by the train of change.

There are seven costly categories of doing nothing, doing far too little or doing the wrong things in business:

1. Cleaning Up Problems: Waste, Spoilage. Poor controls. Downtime. Lack of employee motivation and activity. Back orders because they were not properly stocked. Supervisory involvement in retracing problems and effecting solutions.

2. Rework: Product recalls. Make good for shoddy or inferior work. Poor location. Regulatory red tape. Excess overhead.

3. Missed Marks: Poor controls on quality. Fallout damage from employees with problems (For example, a substance abuser

negatively impacts 20 people before treatment is applied.)
Under-capitalization. Unsuccessful marketing. Unprofitable
pricing.

4. Damage Control: Crisis management. Lawsuits incurred
because procedures were not upheld. Affirmative action
violations. Violations of OSHA, ADA, EEOC, EPA and other
codes. Disasters due to employee carelessness, safety
violations, oversights, etc. Factors outside your   c o m p a n y
that still impede your ability to do business.

5. Recovery and Restoration: Repairing ethically wrong
actions. Empty activities. Mandated cleanups, corrections
and adaptations. Employee turnover, rehiring and retraining.
Isolated or unrealistic management. Bad advice from the
wrong consultants. Repairing a damaged company reputation.

6. Retooling and Restarting: Misuse of company resources,
notably its people. Converting to existing codes and
standards. Chasing the wrong leads, prospects or markets.
Damage caused by inertia or lack of progress. The antichange
"business as usual" philosophy. Long-term expenses incurred
by adopting quick fixes.

7. Opportunity Costs: Failure to understand what business
they're really in. Inability to read the warning signs or
understand external influences. Failure to change. Inability
to plan. Overdependence upon one product or service line.
Diversifying beyond the scope of company expertise. Lack of
an articulated, well-implemented vision.

These are the seven primary factors of The High Cost of Doing
Nothing™ :
1. Failure to value and optimize true company
   resources.
2. Poor premises, policies, processes, procedures,
   precedents and planning.
3. Opportunities not heeded or capitalized.
4. The wrong people, in the wrong jobs. Under-
   trained employees.

5. The wrong consultants (miscast, untrained, improperly used).
6. Lack of articulated focus and vision. With no plan, no journey will be completed.
7. Lack of movement really means falling behind the pack and eventually losing ground.

CHAPTER 11

Self Esteem, Confidence and Reliance
Simplicity
Statistics
Strength
Stress, Worry, Pain
Substance, Depth
Success
Survival

SELF ESTEEM, CONFIDENCE AND RELIANCE

"If I am not for myself, who is for me?"

- Hillel

"To love oneself is the beginning of a life-long romance."

- Oscar Wilde

"To thine own self be true. And it must follow, as the night the day, thou canst not then be false to any man. Our remedies oft in ourselves do lie. We know what we are, but know not what we may be."

- William Shakespeare

"To know oneself is not necessarily to improve oneself. To enter one's own self, it is necessary to go armed to the teeth."

- Paul Valery

"Every man is his own worst enemy. God helps them that help themselves. He helps little that helps not himself. He travels fastest who travels alone."

- Proverbs

"It is better to die on your feet than live on your knees."

- Dolores Ibarrruri

"When people do not respect us, we are sharply offended. Yet deep down in his heart, no man much respects himself."

- Mark Twain

"If you want a thing done well, do it yourself."

- Napoleon Bonaparte

"If the hill will not come to Mahomet, Mahomet will come to the hill."

- Sir Francis Bacon

"I am the master of my fate. I am the captain of my soul."
- W.F. Henley

"If you can keep your head when all about you are losing theirs and blaming it on you. If you can trust yourself when all men doubt you and make allowances for their doubting."
- Rudyard Kipling

"I shall pass through this world but once. If therefore there be any kindness I can show, or any good thing I can do, let me do it now. Let me not defer it or neglect it."
- Etienne de Grellet

SIMPLICITY

"Less is more."
- Robert Browning

"Everything should be made as simple as possible, but not simpler."
- Albert Einstein

"The art of art, the glory of expression, and the sunshine of the light of letters, is simplicity."
- Walt Whitman

"An honest tale speeds best being plainly told. Men of few words are the best men."
- William Shakespeare

"Beauty of style and harmony and grace and good rhythm depend on simplicity."
- Plato

"Seek simplicity, and distrust it."
- Alfred North Whitehead

"Simplicity is the peak of civilization."

- Jessie Sampter

"Manifest plainness. Embrace simplicity. Reduce selfishness. Have few desires."

- Lao-tzu

"It is simplicity that makes the uneducated more effective than the educated when addressing popular audiences."

- Aristotle

"There is a majesty in simplicity which is far above all the quaintness of wit."

- Alexander Pope

"Most modern calendars mar the sweet simplicity of our lives by reminding us that each day that passes is the anniversary of some perfectly uninteresting event."

- Oscar Wilde

"Elegance of language may not be in the power of all of us; but simplicity and straight forwardness are. Write much as you would speak; speak as you think. If with your inferior, speak no coarser than usual; if with your superiors, no finer. Be what you say; and, within the rules of prudence, say what you are."

- Alford

"To be a philosopher is not merely to have subtle thoughts, not even to found a school, but so to love wisdom as to live according to its dictates, a life of simplicity, independence, magnanimity, and trust."

- Henry David Thoreau

Simplicity

In the name of simplicity, here are the key messages to recall from this book and apply toward your business:
- Understand the Big Picture.

- Benefit from Change.
- Avoid False Idols and Facades.
- Remediate the High Costs of Band-Aid Surgery.
- Learning Organizations Are More Successful.
- Plan and Benchmark.
- Craft and Sustain the Vision.

STATISTICS

"Insufficient facts always invites danger."
- *Mr. Spock*, "Star Trek"

"One death is a tragedy. One million deaths are a statistic."
- *Joseph Stalin*

"A little fact is worth a whole limbo of dreams."
- *Ralph Waldo Emerson*

"There are three kinds of lies: lies, damned lies, and statistics."
- *Benjamin Disraeli*

"Smoking is one of the leading causes of statistics."
- *Fletcher Knebel*

"Statistics: The only science that enables different experts using the same figures to draw different conclusions."
- *Evan Esar* , "Esar's Comic Dictionary"

"Learn, compare, collect the facts."
- *Ivan Petrovich Pavlov*

"Let us not underrate the value of a fact. It will one day flower into a truth."
- *Henry David Thoreau*

"Facts do not cease to exist because they are ignored."
- Aldous Huxley

"The statistics on sanity are that one out of every four Americans is suffering from some form of mental illness. Think of your three best friends. If they're okay, then it's you."
- Rita Mae Brown

"Facts are stubborn things, but statistics are more pliable."
- Laurence J. Peter

"Get your facts first, and then you can distort them as much as you please. Statistics show that we lose more fools on this day than on all other days of the year put together. This proves, by the numbers left in stock, that one Fourth of July per year is now inadequate, the country has grown so."
- Mark Twain

"I gather, young man, that you wish to be a Member of Parliament. The first lesson that you must learn is, when I call for statistics about the rate of infant mortality, what I want is proof that fewer babies died when I was Prime Minister than when anyone else was Prime Minister. That is a political statistic."
- Sir Winston Churchill

Statistics

Statistics are indicators of the marketplace in which business must function. By interpreting and examining the research, we can make better informed decisions. Statistics by themselves do no good, unless they are applied to the process of planning an organization's destiny.

Here are some key statistics which illustrate:

Research shows that change is 90% positive and beneficial. Why, then, do many organizations fight what is in their best interest? The average person and organization changes 71% per year. The mastery of change is to benefit from it, rather than become a victim of it.

One-third of the U.S. Gross National Product is sent each year toward cleaning up mistakes, rework, make-goods, corrective action and correcting defects. 92% of all business mistakes may be attributed to poor management decisions. 85% of the time, a formal program of crisis preparedness will help the organization to avert the crisis. One learns three times more from failure than from success. Failures are the surest tracks toward future successes.

50% of the population reads books. 50% do not. Of all high school graduates, 37% will never read another book after formal schooling. Of all college graduates, 16% will never read another book after formal schooling. Thus...a declining overall level of education in our society and serious challenges faced by organizations in training the workforce. 50% of corporate America is functionally illiterate.

Today's work force will require three times the amount of training they now get in order to remain competitive in the future. 29% of the work force wants their boss' job. 70% of corporate CEOs think that business and industry are too much focused on the short-term.

98% of all new business starts are small businesses. 45% of small business owners are children of small business owners. 83% of all domestic companies have fewer than 20 employees. Only 7% of all companies have 100 or more employees.

The current success rate for organizational hires is 14%. If further research is put into looking at the total person and truly fitting the person to the job, then the success rate soars to 75%. That involves testing and more sophisticated hiring practices.

Retaining good employees, involving training, motivation and incentives, is yet another matter. *Employees of organizations steal 10 times more than do shoplifters.
• Employee theft and shoplifting accounting for 15% of the retail cost of merchandise.
  ▪ 35% of employees steal from the company.
  ▪ 28% of those who steal think that they deserve what they take.
  ▪ 21% of those who steal think that the boss can afford the losses.
  ▪ 56% of employees lie to supervisors.
  ▪ 41% of employees falsify records and reports.
  ▪ 31% of the workforce abuses substances.

STRENGTH

"Speak softly and carry a big stick. You will go far."
- African proverb

"A nation does not have to be cruel to be tough. Physical strength can never permanently withstand the impact of spiritual force."
- President Franklin D. Roosevelt

"It is excellent to have a giant's strength, but it is tyrannous to use it like a giant."
- William Shakespeare

"If you can't stand the heat, get out of the kitchen."
- President Harry S. Truman

"The strongest is never strong enough always to be master, unless he transforms strength into right, and obedience into duty."
- Jean Jacques Rousseau

"Know how sublime a thing it is to suffer and be strong."
- Henry Wadsworth Longfellow

"My strength is the strength of ten, because my heart is pure."
- *Alfred, Lord Tennyson*

"This is the Law of the Yukon, that only the strong shall thrive, that surely the weak shall perish, and only the fit survive."
- *Robert William Service*

"Our scientific power has outrun our spiritual power. We have guided missiles and misguided men."
- *Martin Luther King Jr.*, "Strength to Love"

"Rudeness is the weak man's imitation of strength."
- *Eric Hoffer*

"We all have strength enough to endure the misfortunes of others."
- *Francois de La Rochefoucauld*

"The crowd gives the leader new strength. The undertaking of a new action brings new strength."
- *Evenius*

"Let me tell you the secret that has led me to my goal. My strength lies solely in my tenacity."
- *Scientist Louis Pasteur*

"Everyone should carefully observe which way his heart draws him, and then choose that way with all his strength."
- *Hasidic Saying*

"Life only demands from you the strength you possess. Only one feat is possible...not to have run away."
- *Dag Hammarskjold*

"Difficulties strengthen the mind, as labor does the body." Seneca (5 BC-65 AD)"You gain strength, courage and confidence by every experience in which you really stop to look fear in the face. You are able to say to yourself, 'I have lived through this horror. I can take the next thing that comes along.'

You must do the thing you think you cannot do."
- Eleanor Roosevelt

"Look well into thyself. There is a source of strength which will always spring up if thou wilt always look there."
- Marcus Aurelius Antoninus

"Dwell not upon thy weariness, thy strength shall be according to the measure of thy desire."
- Arab Proverb

"Associate with well-mannered persons and your manners will improve. Run around with decent folk and your own decent instincts will be strengthened."
- Stanley Walker

"Be a craftsman in speech that thou mayest be strong, for the strength of one is the tongue, and speech is mightier than all fighting."
- Maxims of Ptahhotep

"Be entirely tolerant or not at all. Follow the good path or the evil one. To stand at the crossroads requires more strength than you possess."
- Heinrich Heine

Strength

Companies say outlandish things in order to garner interest and support. They claim they are bigger and stronger, and prospective customers are to assume that backup systems are equally strong.

Beware of those who thump their chests and crow that their "strength" is the drawing card. Often, it is a false base of power. Beware of these proclamations:

"#1 in Sales." My analysis: #1 for now. Sales rankings constantly change. To buy only because a company hypes that they are #1 is not a valid reason. Buy what you want... from a company that you respect. Also, if they're #1, you're just another sales statistic and customer service will suffer commensurately to the numbers behind whom you must stand in line.

"World Class." My analysis: The organization that claims to be "world class" is trying too hard to be put in the league of others. "World class" is not self-bestowed...it is earned via a long track record.

"Wealth and Riches." My analysis: There are no shortcuts to wealth and riches. Nobody will give away their secrets. Pyramid marketing schemes take advantage of failed hopes and ungrounded wishes. As P.T. Barnum once said, "There's a sucker born every minute."

"The Best." My analysis: There are too many ups and downs in business for this to always be true. This proclamation sets a business up to be attacked or disputed by others. Being successful in the long-run is much more admirable than being temporarily "the best."

"For All Your Needs." My analysis: No product or service fulfills all of a customer's needs. To suggest otherwise is narrow-minded. The more self-assured business makes long lists of what it doesn't do. It knows and relishes its niche, without trying to be all things to all people.

"Our Mission." My analysis: This is a sales ploy. Retailers are motivated by keeping the cash registers ringing. It's unlikely that sales people know what a Mission Statement and the Strategic Planning process are. To confuse sales and Big Picture messages is a travesty.

"Family Tradition." My analysis: If the founder is still active in the business and is accessible to customers, then the reputation is upheld. Dysfunctional family-run businesses reflect dysfunctional families. Hiring blood relatives, in-laws

Hank Moore

and old friends is not always good business. A few pull their share, and others coast on the certainty of nepotism. Research shows the odds are against family businesses going past a second generation, for these and other reasons.

Tradition is a red flag expression because it implies that change has not occurred. Nobody does things exactly as they did in the early days. To say they do is deceptive to customers, employees and the good family name. Tradition and maintaining the status quo are two different concepts. Real tradition is predicated upon change management and steady evolution of the business.

When a company says they are the "Fastest Growing," beware! These circumstances are likely in place, each of which will defeat their claims:

1. Systems are not in place to handle rapid growth...perhaps never were.

2. Their only interest is in booking more new business, rather than taking care of what they've already got.

3. Management is relying upon financial people as the primary source of advice, while ignoring the rest of the picture (90%).

4. Team empowerment suffers. Morale is low or uneven. Commitment from workers drops because no corporate culture was created or sustained.

5. Customer service suffers during fast-growth periods. They have to back-pedal and recover customer confidence by doing surveys. Even with results of deteriorating customer service, growth-track companies pay lip service to really fixing their own problems.

6. People do not have the same Vision as the company founder... who has likely not taken enough time to fully develop a Vision and obtain buy-in from others.

250

7. The company founder remains arrogant and complacent, losing touch with marketplace realities and changing conditions.

═══ STRESS, WORRY, PAIN ═══

"Time heals old pain, while it creates new ones."
- Hebrew proverb

"What deep wounds ever healed without a scar?"
- Lord Byron

"If suffer we must, let's suffer on the heights."
- Victor Hugo

"Every little yielding to anxiety is a step away from the natural heart of man."
- Japanese proverb

"A man who fears suffering is already suffering from what he fears."
- Michel de Montaigne

"A trouble shared is a trouble halved. Don't meet troubles halfway. An hour of pain is as long as a day of pleasure. He that lives long suffers much. Take things as they come."
- Proverbs

"Nothing begins and nothing ends that is not paid with moan. For we are born in others' pain and perish in our own."
- Francis Thompson

"Over the years, your bodies become walking autobiographies, telling friends and strangers alike of the minor and major stresses of your lives."

- Marilyn Ferguson

"At the worst, a house unkept cannot be so distressing as a life unlived."

- Dame Rose Macaulay

"If you are distressed by anything external, the pain is not due to the thing itself, but to your estimate of it; and this you have the power to revoke at any moment."

- Marcus Aurelius Antoninus

"Indolence is a delightful but distressing state; we must be doing something to be happy."

- Mahatma Gandhi

"Throw out an alarming alarm clock. If the ring is loud and strident, you're waking up to instant stress. You shouldn't be bullied out of bed, just reminded that it's time to start your day."

- Sharon Gold

"The superior man is satisfied and composed. The mean man is always full of distress."

- Confucius, "The Confucian Analects"

"Like all weak men, he laid an exaggerated stress on not changing one's mind."

- W. Somerset Maugham, "Of Human Bondage"

"Small minds are much distressed by little things. Great minds see them all but are not upset by them."

- Francois de La Rochefoucauld

"Music is a discipline, and a mistress of order and good manners, she makes the people milder and gentler, more moral and more reasonable."

- Martin Luther

"The harder the conflict, the more glorious the triumph. What we obtain too cheap, we esteem too lightly; it is dearness only that gives everything its value. I love the man that can smile in trouble, that can gather strength from distress and grow brave by reflection. 'Tis the business of   little minds to shrink; but he whose heart is firm, and whose conscience approves his conduct, will pursue his principles unto death. The real man smiles in trouble, gathers strength from distress, and grows brave by reflection."

- Thomas Paine

"He who endeavors to serve, to benefit and improve the world, is like a swimmer who struggles against a rapid current in a river lashed into angry waves by the winds.
Often they roar over his head, often they beat him back and baffle him. Most men yield to the stress of the current. The stout, strong heart and vigorous arms struggle on toward ultimate success."

- Albert Pike

"What a distressing contrast there is between the radiant intelligence of the child and the feeble mentality of the average adult."

- Sigmund Freud

"I was much distressed by next door people who had twin babies and played the violin; but one of the twins died, and the other has eaten the fiddle - so all is peace."

- Edward Lear

"When anyone asks me how I can best describe my experience in nearly forty years at sea, I merely say, uneventful. Of course there have been winter gales, and storms and fog and the like. But in all my experience, I have never been in any accident...or any sort worth speaking about. I have seen but one vessel in distress in all my years at sea. I never saw a wreck and never have been wrecked nor was I ever in any predicament that threatened to end in disaster of any sort."

- E. J. Smith

═══ **SUBSTANCE, DEPTH** ═══

"Those who go beneath the surface do so at their own peril."
- Oscar Wilde

"I detest that man who hides one thing in the depths of his heart, and speaks for another."
- Homer

"Do not judge men by mere appearances; for the light laughter that bubbles on the lip often mantles over the depths of sadness, and the serious look may be the sober veil that covers a divine peace and joy."
- E. H. Chapin

"You can't do anything about the length of your life, but you can do something about its width and depth."
- Evan Esar

"The most wonderful of all things in life, I believe, is the discovery of another human being with whom one's relationship has a glowing depth, beauty, and joy as the years increase. This inner progressiveness of love between two human beings is a most marvelous thing, it cannot be found by looking for it or by passionately wishing for it."
- Sir Hugh Walpoe

"The difference between a rut and a grave is the depth."
- Gerald Burrill

"Do not hover always on the surface of things, nor take up suddenly, with mere appearances; but penetrate into the depth of matters, as far as your time and circumstances allow, especially in those things which relate to your profession."
- Isaac Watts

"A little philosophy inclineth man's mind to atheism. But depth in philosophy bringeth men's minds about to religion."

- Sir Francis Bacon

"Never offend people with style when you can offend them with substance."

- Sam Brown

"The meeting of two personalities is like the contact of two chemical substances: if there is any reaction, both are transformed."

- Carl Jung

"Beware lest you lose the substance by grasping at the shadow."

- Aesop

"The very essence of literature is the war between emotion and intellect, between life and death. When literature becomes too intellectual—when it begins to ignore the passions, the motions—it becomes sterile, silly, and actually without substance."

- Isaac Bashevis Singer

"I prepared excitedly for my departure, as if this journey had a mysterious significance. I had decided to change my mode of life. "'til now," I told myself, "you have only seen the shadow and been well content with it; now, I am going to lead you into the substance."

- Nikos Kazantzakis, Zorba the Greek

"The demonstration that no possible combination of known substances, known forms of machinery and known forms of force, can be united in a practical machine by which man shall fly long distances through the air, seems to the writer as complete as it is possible for the demonstration of any physical fact to be."

- Simon Newcomb

"Half the controversies in the world are verbal ones; and could they be brought to a plain issue they would be brought to a prompt termination. Parties engaged in them would then perceive either that in substance they agreed together, or that their difference was one of first principles. We need not dispute, we need not prove, we need but define. At all events, let us, if we can, do this first of all and then see who are left for us to dispute; what is left for us to prove."

- Cardinal John Newman

"Creative power, is that receptive attitude of expectancy which makes a mold into which the plastic and undifferentiated substance can flow and take the desired form."

- Thomas Troward

SUCCESS

"There are no gains without pains."
Adlai Stevenson

"The desire for fame tempts even noble minds."
St. Augustine

"Success produces success, just as money produces money."
Sebastian R.N. Chamfort

"Fame is like a river, that beareth up things light and swollen, and drowns things weighty and solid."
Sir Francis Bacon

"Fame is a bee. It has a song. It has a sting. Ah, too, it has a wing."
Emily Dickinson

"Oh how quickly the world's glory passes away."
Thomas A. Kempis

"Be nice to people on your way up because you'll need them on your way down."
Wilson Mizner

"Success has killed more men than bullets."
Texas Guinan

"Nothing succeeds like success."
Proverb

"The penalty of success is to be bored by people who used to snub you."
Nancy Astor

"Success is counted sweetest by those who never succeed."
Emily Dickinson

"Success is relative. It is what we can make of the mess we have made of things."
T.S. Eliot

"There are two reasons why I am successful in show business, and I am standing on both of them."
Betty Grable

"Victory has a thousand fathers, but defeat is an orphan."
President John F. Kennedy

"There are two tragedies in life. One is to lose your heart's desire. The other is to gain it."
George Bernard Shaw

"There is always room at the top."

- Daniel Webster

"Fame can never make us lie down contentedly on a deathbed."

- Alexander Pope

"Success is like a liberation or the first phase of a love affair."

- Jeanne Moreau

"The secret of my success is that no woman has ever been jealous of me."

- Elsa Maxwell

"What rage for fame attends both great and small. Better be damned than mentioned at all."

- John Wolcot

"The only place where success comes before work is a dictionary."

- Vidal Sassoon

"The only way to succeed is to make people hate you. That way, they remember you."

- Joseph von Sternberg

"There is only one success, to be able to spend your life in your own way."

- Christopher Morley

"If you think you can win, you can win. Faith is necessary to victory."

- William Hazlitt

Success

Here are my suggested ingredients of success:

1. Finding knowledge in new and unique ways. Strive to learn something new everyday. Learn from examples (good and bad). Education leads to knowledge, which leads to wisdom. Develop continuing education, professional development and life philosophies.

2. Doing work that you're proud of. No matter what the job title, task or career orientation, work can be done professionally. If it doesn't mean something to you, it will not contribute to the marketplace or society at large. When you value it, they will begin to reciprocate.

3. Developing a philosophy...individually and organizationally. Analyze where you've been. Evaluate strengths and weaknesses. Analyze and strategize opportunities. Establish bigger goals this year than you had last year...with means and reasons for reaching them.

4. Handling mistakes and crises. Everyone makes mistakes. The mark of Quality is how you handle them. Learn the art of diagnosing problems, taking input and effecting workable solutions. Planning for crises will divert them from occurring, 85% of the time. Waiting until the last moment to apply "band-aid surgery" is self-defeating and costly.

5. Dealing with fear. Everyone has fear. Those who deny it the most are detrimental to your success and that of your organization. Understand fears, and set plans to work with them. Remove barriers to success. Turn internal fears into motivating forces. Fears will never go away⊠but can facilitate the path toward success.

6. Learning to read others' screens. Put yourself in other people's shoes, and communicate in their sphere...to achieve desired actions-results. Learn what motivates others and

colors their take on life...in order to work well with diverse peoples and organizational cultures.

7. Self fulfillment, purpose and commitment. Career-Life Vision, Body of Work. Develop a strategic plan, core values and action steps to accomplish your dreams. While others may roam aimlessly through life, you will achieve, sustain and share success. Commit to and thrive upon change.

SURVIVAL

"If you care to drive, drive with care. Leave blood at the Red Cross, not on the highway. On the road, it's not who's right that counts...it's who's left."

- Broderick Crawford

"It isn't important to come out on top. What matters is to be the one who comes out alive."

- Bertolt Brecht

"Happiness in the ordinary sense is not what one needs in life, though one is right to aim at it. The true satisfaction is to come through and see those whom one loves come through."

- E.M. Forster

"People are inexterminable, like flies and bed-bugs. There will always be some that survive in cracks and crevices."

- Robert Frost

"One can survive everything nowadays, except death."

- Oscar Wilde

"When you get to the end of your rope, tie a knot and hang on."

- Franklin D. Roosevelt

CHAPTER 12

Tact
Talent/Potential
Tax
Teamwork, Collaborations, Partnering
Technology
Temptation
Thinking
Time
Trust, Relationship Building
Truth, Understanding

TACT

"Leave well alone. Let sleeping dogs lie."

- Proverbs

"Tact consists in knowing how far we may go too far."

-Jean Cocteau

"One shouldn't talk of halters in the hanged man's house."

- Miguel de Cervantes

"Although there exist many thousand subjects for elegant conversation, there are persons who cannot meet a cripple without talking about feet."

- Chinese proverb

"Tact is a valuable attribute in gaining practice. It consists in telling a squint-eyed man that he has a fine, firm chin."

- J. Chalmers Da Costa

"Competence, like truth, beauty and contact lenses, is in the eye of the beholder."

- Laurence J. Peter, "The Peter Principle"

"Tact is the ability to describe others as they see themselves."

- President Abraham Lincoln

"Sometimes I think the surest sign that intelligent life exists elsewhere in the universe is that none of it has tried to contact us."

- Bill Watterson, "Calvin and Hobbes"

"A happy childhood is poor preparation for human contacts."

- Colette

"Lying increases the creative faculties, expands the ego, and lessens the frictions of social contacts."

- Clare Booth Luce

"Tact is the knack of making a point without making an enemy."
- Isaac Newton

"It is an illusion that youth is happy, an illusion of those who have lost it. The young know they are wretched for they are full of the truthless ideal which have been instilled into them, and each time they come in contact with the real, they are bruised and wounded."

- W. Somerset Maugham

"Don't flatter yourself that friendship authorizes you to say disagreeable things to your intimates. The nearer you come with a person, the more necessary do tact and courtesy become. Except in cases of necessity, leave your friend to learn unpleasant things from his enemies; they are ready enough to tell them."

- Supreme Court Justice Oliver Wendell Holmes

"The meeting of two personalities is like the contact of two chemical substances. If there is any reaction, both are transformed."

- Carl Jung

"Step with care and great tact. And remember that Life's a Great Balancing Act. Just never forget to be dexterous and deft. And never mix up your right foot with your left."
- Dr. Suess, "Oh, the Places You'll Go"

"The creative act is not performed by the artist alone. The spectator brings the work in contact with the external world by deciphering and interpreting its inner qualifications and thus adds his contribution to the creative act."

- Marcel Duchamp

"Tact is, after all, a kind of mind reading."

- Sarah Orne Jewett

"A family is a place where minds come in contact with one another. If these minds love one another the home will be

as beautiful as a flower garden. But if these minds get out of harmony with one another it is like a storm that plays havoc with the garden."
- *Buddha*

━━━ TALENT/POTENTIAL ━━━

"Talent develops in quiet places, character in the full current of human life."

- Goethe

"There is no substitute for talent. Industry and all the virtues are of no avail."

- Aldous Huxley

"Middle age snuffs out more talent than ever wars or sudden death do."

- Richard Hughes

"It's not enough to be Hungarian. You must have talent too."
- Alexander Korda

"Let our children grow tall, and some taller than others if they have it in them to do so."

- Margaret Thatcher

"I am no more humble than my talents require."
- Oscar Levant

"Getting ahead in a difficult profession requires avid faith in yourself. That is why some people with mediocre talent, but with great inner drive, go much further than people with vastly superior talent."

- Sophia Loren

"The government consists of a gang of men exactly like you

and me. They have, taking one with another, no special talent for the business of government; they have only a talent for getting and holding office."
- H. L. Mencken

"It took me 15 years to discover that I had no talent for writing, but I couldn't give it up because by that time I was too famous."
- Robert Benchley

"Mediocrity knows nothing higher than itself. Talent instantly recognizes genius."
- Sir Arthur Conan Doyle, "Sherlock Holmes, Valley of Fear"

"There are admirable potentialities in every human being. Believe in your strength and your youth. Learn to repeat endlessly to yourself, 'It all depends on me.'"
-Andre Gide

"Man's main task in life is to give birth to himself, to become what he potentially is."
- Erich Fromm

"It seems to me that people have vast potential. Most people can do extraordinary things if they have the confidence or take the risks. Yet most people don't. They sit in front of the telly and treat life as if it goes on forever."
- Philip Adams

"Engineering is the science of economy, of conserving the energy, kinetic and potential, provided and stored up by nature for the use of man. It is the business of engineering to utilize this energy to the best advantage, so that there may be the least possible waste."
- William A. Smith

"The engineer is the key figure in the material progress of the world. It is his engineering that makes a reality of the potential value of science by translating scientific knowledge into tools, resources, energy and labor to bring them into the service of man. To make contributions of this kind the engineer requires the imagination to visualize the needs of society and to appreciate what is possible as well as the technological and broad social age understanding to bring his vision to reality."

- Sir Eric Ashby

"If I have ever made any valuable discoveries, it has been owing more to patient attention, than to any other talent."

- Isaac Newton

"Press on. Nothing in the world can take the place of perseverance. Talent will not; nothing is more common than unsuccessful men with talent. Genius will not. Unrewarded genius is almost a proverb. Education will not. The world is full of educated derelicts. Persistence and determination alone are omnipotent."

- President Calvin Coolidge

"Man is the victim of the very instruments he values most. Every gain in power, every mastery of natural forces, every scientific addition to knowledge, has proved potentially dangerous, because it has not been accompanied by equal gains in self-understanding."

- Lewis Mumford

"I don't measure America by its achievement but by its potential."

- Shirley Chisholm

"You must keep sending work out; you must never let a manuscript do nothing but eat its head off in a drawer. You send that work out again and again, while you're working on another one. If you have talent, you will receive some success, but only if you persist."

- Isaac Asimov

"The toughest thing about success is that you've got to keep on being a success. Talent is only a starting point in this business. You've got to keep on working that talent. Someday I'll reach

for it and it won't be there."
- Irving Berlin

"Toil to make yourself remarkable by some talent or other."
- Seneca

"Whatever you are by nature, keep to it; never desert your line of talent. Be what nature intended you for and you will succeed."
- Sydney Smith

"If you have a talent, use it in every which way possible. Don't hoard it. Don't dole it out like a miser. Spend it lavishly like a millionaire intent on going broke."
- Brendan Francis

"Hide not your talents, they for use were made. What's a sundial in the shade?"
- Benjamin Franklin

"Everyone has talent. What is rare is the courage to follow the talent to the dark place where it leads."
- Erica Jong

TAX

"Taxation without representation is tyranny."
- James Otis

"Taxes are what we pay for a civilized society."
- Supreme Court Justice Oliver Wendell Holmes

"The hardest thing in the world to understand is income tax."
- Albert Einstein

"The taxpayer is someone who works for the federal government but doesn't have to take a civil service examination."

- President Ronald Reagan

"The wisdom of man never yet contrived a system of taxation that operates with perfect equality."

- President Andrew Jackson

"In this world, nothing can be said to be certain except death and taxes."

- Benjamin Franklin

"The income tax has made liars out of the American people more than golf has."

- Will Rogers

"Taxes are dues that we pay for the privileges of membership in an organized society."

- President Franklin D. Roosevelt

TEAMWORK, COLLABORATIONS, PARTNERING

"All for one, one for all."

- Alexandre Dumas

"Never ask that which you are not prepared to give."

- Apache law

"Tsze-Kung asked, saying, 'Is there one word which may serve as a rule of practice for all one's life?" The Master said, "Is not Reciprocity such a word? What you do not want done to yourself, do not do to others."

- Confucius

"Whose bread I eat, his song I sing."

- German proverb

"A chain is no stronger than its weakest link. Union is strength. United we stand, divided we fall."

- Proverbs

"It takes more than one to make a ballet."

- Ninette de Valois

"What I want is men who will support me when I am in the wrong."

- Lord Melbourne

"There are only two forces that unite men: fear and interest."
- Napoleon Bonaparte

"When bad men combine, the good must associate. Else they will fall, one by one, an unpitied sacrifice in a contemptible struggle."

- Edmund Burke

"One man alone can be pretty dumb sometimes, but for real bona fide stupidity, there ain't nothin' can beat teamwork."
- Edward Abbey

"The finest plans have always been spoiled by the littleness of those that should carry them out. Even emperors can't do it all by themselves."

- Bertolt Brecht

"Everyone has observed how much more dogs are animated when they hunt in a pack, than when they pursue their game apart. We might, perhaps, be at a loss to explain this phenomenon, if we had not experience of a similar in ourselves."
- David Hume

Teamwork, Collaborations, Partnering

The biggest source of growth and increased opportunities in today's business climate lie in the way that individuals and companies work together.

It is becoming increasingly rare to find an individual or organization that has not yet been required to team with others. Lone rangers and sole-source providers simply cannot succeed in competitive environments and global economies. Those who benefit from collaborations, rather than become the victim of them, will log the biggest successes in business years ahead.

Here are my definitions of three terms of teamwork, intended to help by differentiating their intended objectives:

Collaborations --- Parties willingly cooperating together. Working jointly with others, especially in an intellectual pursuit. Cooperation with an instrumentality with which one is not immediately connected.

Partnering --- A formal relationship between two or more associates. Involves close cooperation among parties, with each having specified and joint rights and responsibilities.

Joint-Venturing --- Partners come together for specific purposes or projects that may be beyond the scope of individual members. Each retains individual identity. The joint-venture itself has its own identity...reflecting favorably upon work to be done and upon the partners.

I have observed the greatest successes with collaborations, partnering and joint-ventures to occur when:
- Crisis or urgent need forced the client to hire a consortium.
- Time deadlines and nature of the project required a cohesive team approach.
- The work required multiple professional skills.

- Consortium members were tops in their fields.
- Consortium members truly understood teamwork and had prior successful experiences in joint-venturing.
- Consortium members wanted to learn from each other.
- Early successes spurred future collaborations.
- Joint-venturing was considered an ongoing process, not a "once in awhile" action.
- Each team member realized something of value.
- The client recommended the consortium to others.

My own disappointments with previous collaborations include:
- Failure of participants to understand—and thus utilize—each other's talents.
- One or more participants have had one or a few bad experiences and tend to over-generalize about the worth of consortiums.
- One partner puts another down on the basis of academic credentials or some professional designation that sets themselves apart from other team members.
- Participants exhibit the "Lone Ranger" syndrome... preferring the comfort of trusting the one person they have counted upon.
- Participants exhibit the "I can do that" syndrome, thinking that they do the same exact things that other consortium members do and, thus, see no value in working together, sharing projects and referring business.
- Junior associates of consortium members want to hoard the billing dollars in-house to look good to their superiors, enhance their billable quotas or fulfill other objectives that they are not sophisticated enough to identify.
- Junior associates of consortium members refuse to recognize seniority and wisdom of senior associates, utilizing the power of the budget to control creative thoughts and strategic thinking of subcontractors.

Here are the reasons to give the concepts of Collaborating, Partnering and Joint-Venturing a chance:
- Think of the "ones that got away," the opportunities that a team could have created.
- Think of contracts that were awarded to others who exhibited a team approach.
- Learn from industries where consortiums are the rule, rather than the exception (space, energy, construction, high-tech, etc.).
- The marketplace is continually changing.
- Subcontractor, supplier, support talent and vendor information can be shared.
- Consortiums are inevitable. If we don't do it early, others will beat us to it.

The benefits for participating principals and firms include:
- Ongoing association and professional exchange with the best in respective fields.
- Utilize professional synergy to create opportunities that individuals could not.
- Serve as a beacon for professionalism.
- Provide access to experts otherwise not known to potential clients.
- Refer and cross-sell each others' services.
- Develop programs and materials to meet new and emerging marketplaces.

TECHNOLOGY

"The machine threatens all achievement."

- Rainer Maria Rilke

"Machines are worshipped because they are beautiful and valued because they confer power. They are hated because

they are hideous and loathed because they impose slavery."
- Bertrand Russell

"Any sufficiently advanced technology is indistinguishable from magic."
- Arthur C. Clarke

"Give me a firm place to stand, and I will move the earth."
- Archimedes

"Man is a tool-using animal."
- Thomas Carlyle

"The new electronic interdependence recreates the world in the image of a global village. For tribal man, space was the uncontrollable mystery. For technological man, it is time that occupies the same role."
- Marshall McLuhan

"The machine does not isolate man from the great problems of nature but plunges him more deeply into them."
- Antoine de Saint-Exupery

"Our scientific power has outrun our spiritual power. We have guided missiles and misguided men."
- Martin Luther King, Jr.

"Technology: the knack of so arranging the world that we don't have to experience it."
- Max Frisch

"The real problem is not whether machines think, but whether men do."
- B.F. Skinner

"No man who has wrestled with a self-adjusting card table can ever quite be the man he once was."
- James Thurber

Technology

Technology is important....but not the most important part of running an organization. We must learn how to use it in order to put it into perspective.

Technology constitutes one-tenth of 1% of any organization's Big Picture. People constitute 28%, and planning activities should constitute 15%. Unfortunately, many companies put their "bells and whistles" behind technology, while ignoring the other 99.9%. That sets technology up as both a false god and a scapegoat, neither of which is fair or accurate.

Technology must be put into proper business contexts. It is a tool of the trade...not an organizational philosophy. It constitutes one small portion of business equipment.

Technology is kept in the hands of a small few in most organizations, though everyone should develop a functional knowledge of it. Minds that utilize it must be stimulated, trained and rewarded. Technology is not a mind by itself. It reflects the need for changes in business...but cannot facilitate improvements by itself. Even companies whose core product is technology need to put most of their emphasis upon producing products and getting them to market.

Often, technology is a "bells and whistles" project that companies readily put money behind, rather than first addressing total-organizational issues, problems and opportunities. It does not solve all problems, nor should it be blamed for creating all problems.

To many, technology is still "fun and games" and is not fully utilized as a productivity tool. The more that we learn it, the more that technology works. The focus always needs to go back to understanding what business you're really in, what you become, how you exist and many other unanswered questions. Applying "band-aid surgery" is not the answer and is more costly in the long-run.

People need more than technology to be productive. Yet, without adequate technology, they are handicapped. We must not give a disproportionate amount of attention to technology and leave people (any organization's best resource) the short end of the stick.

Organizations often adopt a "we versus they" attitude toward technology. "We" make the policies and decisions. "They" are the technology providers and implementers, who support us but do not participate in corporate decisions. Often, primarily the rank and file utilizes technology. Management does not see a reason to embrace technology. In minds of many managers, technocrats are not in the decision-making loop. This is an unfortunate flaw of corporate thinking.

Each year, companies spend billions of dollars on the latest technology but do not reward their people for creative thinking. People are trained in the use of technology but are not trained adequately in other aspects of business operation...notably in the powers of reason, communications and the people skills necessary to work optimally with each other.

Shifting paradigms toward accepting modern technology must be accompanied by modified behaviors. Thinking that technology will cure all ills is another version of burying one's head in the sand to the truths around us.

Technology proponents say that those who do not embrace it are dinosaurs, out of touch and computer illiterate...three distinct categories, one of which has to do with technology. Certainly, every executive should learn how to operate a computer. More importantly, technology professionals should learn more management skills and must have more exposure to non-tech aspects of their business.

The bigger priority is to apply creative thinking to all aspects of company operation. Use technology as a tool. Utilize people as the masters of that tool. Encompass planning and bigger-picture thinking into all business operations. Therefore, those who use technology do so with a bigger understanding of its place in the Big Picture.

When technology is thought of as a component in the "macro," rather than a "micro" world unto itself, it will have mature utilization. Otherwise, it will be viewed as a bunch of high-priced toys, which are played out of context to the main game.

TEMPTATION

"I generally avoid temptation unless I can't resist it."

- Mae West

"Tempt not a desperate man. The tempter or the tempted...who sins the most?"

- William Shakespeare

"Good habits result from resisting temptation. Forbidden fruit is sweet. If you can't be good, be careful."

- Proverbs

"I can resist everything except temptation. The only way to get rid of a temptation is to yield to it. Resist it, and your soul grows sick with longing for the things it has forbidden to itself."

- Oscar Wilde

"Saintliness is also a temptation."

- Jean Anouilh

"I never resist temptation because I have found that things that are bad for me never tempt me. Virtue is insufficient temptation."

- George Bernard Shaw

"Most people would like to be delivered from temptation but would like it to keep in touch."
- Robert Orben

"It is good to be without vices, but it is not good to be without temptations."
- Walter Bagehot

"Those who flee temptation generally leave a forwarding address."
- Lane Olinghouse

"There are several good protections against temptations, but the surest is cowardice."
- Mark Twain

"There is not any memory with less satisfaction than the memory of some temptation we resisted."
- James Branch Cabell

"Temptation rarely comes in working hours. It is in their leisure time that men are made or marred."
- W. N. Taylor

"We live in a time of transition, an uneasy era which is likely to endure for the rest of this century. During the period we may be tempted to abandon some of the time-honored principles and commitments which have been proven during the difficult times of past generations. We must never yield to this temptation. Our American values are not luxuries, but necessities—not the salt in our bread, but the bread itself."
- President Jimmy Carter

"The last temptation is the greatest treason: to do the right deed for the wrong reason."
- T. S. Eliot

"Why comes temptation, but for man to meet and master and

crouch beneath his foot, and so be pedestaled in triumph?"
- Robert Browning

"Blessed is the man that endureth temptation: for when he is tried, he shall receive the crown of life."
- Bible, James 1:12

"Most people would like to be delivered from temptation but would like it to keep in touch."
- Robert Orben

"The devil made me do it."
- Flip Wilson

THINKING

"If two men agree on everything, you may be sure that one of them is doing the thinking."
- President Lyndon B. Johnson

"The man whose second thoughts are good is worth watching."
- J.M. Barrie

"Many people would sooner die than think. In fact, they do."
- Bertrand Russell

"I think. Therefore, I am."
- Rene Descartes

"The most fluent talkers or most plausible reasoners are not always the justest thinkers."
- William Hazlitt

"Most of one's life is one prolonged effort to prevent oneself from thinking."
- Aldous Huxley

"There is nothing either good or bad, but thinking makes it so."
- *William Shakespeare*

"Discovery consists of seeing what everybody has seen and thinking what nobody has thought."
- *Albert von Szent-Gyorgyi,* "Irving Good, The Scientist Speculates"

"Aristotle was famous for knowing everything. He taught that the brain exists to cool the blood and is not involved in the process of thinking. This is true only of certain persons."
- *Will Cuppy*

"The significant problems we have cannot be solved at the same level of thinking with which we created them."
- *Albert Einstein*

"A good listener is usually thinking about something else. Classical music is the kind we keep thinking will turn into a tune."
- *Kin Hubbard*

"There is no expedient to which a man will not go to avoid the labor of thinking."
- *Thomas A. Edison*

"Words ought to be a little wild for they are the assaults of thought on the unthinking."
- *John Maynard Keynes*

"Few people think more than two or three times a year. I have made an international reputation for myself by thinking once or twice a week."
- *George Bernard Shaw*

"Too many people are thinking of security instead of opportunity. They seem more afraid of life than death."
- *James F. Byrnes*

"The important thing in science is not so much to obtain new facts as to discover new ways of thinking about them."
- Sir William Bragg

"There are two ways to slide easily through life; to believe everything or to doubt everything. Both ways save us from thinking."
- Alfred Korzybski

"If you make people think they're thinking, they'll love you. But if you really make them think, they'll hate you."
- Don Marquis

TIME

"To choose time is to save time."
- Sir Francis Bacon

"Time keeps on slipping into the future."
- Steve Miller Band

"Men talk of killing time, while time quietly kills them."
- Dion Boucicault

"Dost thou love life? Then do not squander time, for that's the stuff life is made of. Time is money."
- Benjamin Franklin

"Time is a great teacher. Unfortunately, it kills all its pupils."
- Hector Berlioz

"Time present and time past are both perhaps present in time future, and time future contained in time past."
- T.S. Eliot

"I must govern the clock, not be governed by it."
- Golda Meir

"An hour in the morning is worth two in the evening. There are only 24 hours in a day. There is a time and place for everything. Time and tide wait for no man. Time cures the sick man, not the ointment. Time is a great healer. Time will tell."

- Proverbs

"Time ripens all things. No man is born wise."

- Cervantes, "Don Quixote"

"Time is the great physician."

- Benjamin Disraeli

"Come what come may. Time and the hour runs through the roughest day. I wasted time, and now doth time waste me."

- William Shakespeare

"Time eases all things."

- Sophocles

"The now, the here, through which all future plunges to the past."

- James Joyce

"Time wounds all heals."

- Groucho Marx

"We must use time as a tool, not a couch."

- President John F. Kennedy

"As if you could kill time without injuring eternity."

- Henry David Thoreau

"Take care of the minutes, for hours will take care of themselves."

- Earl of Chesterfield

TRUST, RELATIONSHIP BUILDING

"If I have the public trust, then anything is possible. If I don't have it, then nothing is possible."
- President Abraham Lincoln

"A friendship founded on business is better than a business founded on friendship."
- John D. Rockefeller

"The body is shaped, disciplined, honored, and in time, trusted."
- Martha Graham

"I know God will not give me anything I can't handle. I just wish that He didn't trust me so much."
- Mother Teresa

"Trust men and they will be true to you; treat them greatly, and they will show themselves great."
- Ralph Waldo Emerson

"Love all, trust a few. Do wrong to none."
- William Shakespeare

"Just trust yourself, then you will know how to live."
- Johann Wolfgang von Goethe

"Put more trust in nobility of character than in an oath."
- Solon

"Never trust the advice of a man in difficulties."
- Aesop

"Love God and trust your feelings. Be loyal to them. Don't betray them."
- Robert C. Pollock

"If you wish in this world to advance, your merits you're bound to enhance. You must stir it and stump it, and blow your own trumpet, or trust me, you haven't a chance."

- W. S. Gilbert

"Do not trust all men, but trust men of worth. The former course is silly, the latter a mark of prudence."

- Democritus

"A human being is only interesting if he's in contact with himself. I learned you have to trust yourself, be what you are, and do what you ought to do the way you should do it. You have got to discover you, what you do, and trust it."

- Barbra Streisand

Trust, Relationship Building

These are the seven stages of relationship building among collaborators and partners in business:

1. Want to Get Business. Seeking rub-off effect, success by association. Sounds good to the marketplace. Nothing ventured, nothing gained. Why not try!

2. Want to Garner Ideas. Learn more about the customer. Each team member must commit to professional development... taking the program to a higher level. Making sales calls (mandated or voluntarily) does not constitute relationship building.

3. First Attempts. Conduct programs that get results, praise, requests for more. To succeed, it needs to be more than an advertising and direct marketing campaign.

4. Mistakes, Successes & Lessons. Competition, marketplace changes or urgent need led the initiative to begin. Customer retention and enhancement program requires a cohesive team

approach and multiple talents.

5. Continued Collaborations. Collaborators truly understand teamwork and had prior successful experiences at customer service. The sophisticated ones are skilled at building and utilizing colleagues and outside experts.

6. Want and Advocate Teamwork. Team members want to learn from each other. All share risks equally. Early successes inspire deeper activity. Business relationship building is considered an ongoing process, not a "once in awhile" action or marketing gimmick.

7. Commitment to the Concept and Each Other. Each team member realizes something of value. Customers recommend and freely refer business to the institution. What benefits one partner benefits all.

═ TRUTH, UNDERSTANDING ═

"Hell is truth seen too late."

- Tryon Edwards

"When you have eliminated the impossible, whatever remains, however improbable, must be the truth."

- Sir Arthur Conan Doyle

"And the lonely voice of youth cries, What Is Truth?"

- Johnny Cash

"We swallow greedily any lie that flatters us, but we sip only little by little at a truth we find bitter. I can be expected to look for the truth, but not to find it."

- Denis Diderot

"The truth is always modern, and there never comes a time

when it is safe to give it voice."

- Clarence Darrow

"Truth crushed to earth shall rise again."

- William Cullen Bryant

"Tis strange but true. For truth is always strange...stranger than fiction."

- Lord Byron

"Truth is the only ground to stand upon."

- Elizabeth Cady Stanton

"Truth is the beginning of every good thing, both in heaven and on earth. And he who be blessed and happy should be from the first a partaker of truth, for then he can be trusted."

- Plato

"It is the customary fate of new truths to begin as heresies and to end as superstitions."

- T.H. Huxley

"A great truth is a truth whose opposite is also a truth."

- Thomas Mann

"There is nothing so powerful as truth...and nothing so strange."

- Daniel Webster

"Better a lie that heals than a truth that wounds. Many a true word is spoken in jest. Tell the truth, and shame the devil. Truth fears no trial. Truth is stranger than fiction. Truth will out."

- Proverbs

"Let us begin by committing ourselves to the truth, to see it like it is and to tell it like it is, to find the truth, to speak the truth and live with the truth."

- Richard M. Nixon

"Truth is no road to fortune."

- Jean Jacques Rousseau

"I never give them hell. I just tell the truth, and they think it's hell."

- Harry S. Truman

"Truth is mighty and will prevail. There is nothing the matter with this, except that it ain't so."

- Mark Twain

"Truth confronts us, and we can no longer understand anything."

- Paul Valery

"Truth is on the march. Nothing can stop it now."

- Emile Zola

"The highest result of education is tolerance." Helen Keller "Live and let live."

- Scottish proverb

"Live and let die."

- Ian Fleming

"All truth passes through three stages. First, it is ridiculed. Second, it is violently opposed. Third, it is accepted as being self-evident."

- Arthur Schopenhauer

"The most comprehensible thing about the world is that any of it is incomprehensible."

- Albert Einstein

"No law or ordinance is mightier than understanding."

- Plato

"Thought must be divided against itself before it can come to any knowledge of itself."

- Aldous Huxley

"Much learning does not teach understanding."

- Heraclitus

"The people may be made to follow a course of action, but they may not be made to understand it."

- Confucius

"Everything that irritates us about others can lead us to an understanding of ourselves."

- Carl Jung

"It is well to give when asked but it is better to give unasked, through understanding."

- Kahlil Gibran

"The family is changing not disappearing. We have to broaden our understanding of it, look for the new metaphors."

- Mary Catherine Bateson

"Beginning today, treat everyone you meet as if they were going to be dead by midnight. Extend them all the care, kindness and understanding you can muster. Your life will never be the same again."

- Og Mandino, "The Greatest Miracle in the World"

"The medium is the message."

- Marshall McLuhan, "Understanding Media"

"Boredom is a sign of satisfied ignorance, blunted apprehension, crass sympathies, dull understanding, feeble powers of attention, and irreclaimable weakness of character."

- James Bridie

"The important thing is to know when to laugh, or since laughing is somewhat undignified to smile. But the smile must be of the right kind must have understanding in it, and friendliness, and a good deal of patience."

- Roderic Owen

"Their understanding begins to swell and the approaching tide will shortly fill the reasonable shores that now lie foul and muddy."

- William Shakespeare

"I have found you an argument. I am not obliged to find you an understanding."

- James Boswell

"Modern Man is the victim of the very instruments he values most. Every gain in power, every mastery of natural forces, every scientific addition to knowledge, has proved potentially dangerous, because it has not been accompanied by equal gains in self-understanding and self-discipline."

- Lewis Mumford

CHAPTER 13

Values, Ideals
Vision
Work
Youth

VALUES, IDEALS

"You get what you pay for."

- Proverb

"If you believe in an ideal, you don't own it. It owns you."
- Raymond Chandler

"A cynic is a man who knows the price of everything and the value of nothing."

- Oscar Wilde

"There ain't a wrong man in the world who can stand up against a right man who knows he is right and keeps on a-comin."
- Lash Larue

"Good merchandise, even when hidden, soon finds buyers."
- Plautus

"Things are only worth what you make them worth."
- Moliere

"Let it be."

- John Lennon

"Imagine there's no heaven. It's easy if you try. No help below us. Above us only sky. Imagine all the people living for today."
- John Lennon

"A radical is a man with both feet firmly planted in the air."
- President Franklin D. Roosevelt

"Failure comes only when we forget our ideals and objectives and principles."

- Jawaharal Nehru

"Ideals are like stars; you will not succeed in touching them with your hands. But like the seafaring man on the desert of waters, you choose them as your guides, and following them you will reach your destiny."

- Carl Schurz

"Some have half-baked ideas because their ideals are not heated up enough."

- Anonymous

"People love high ideals, but they got to be about thirty-three percent plausible."

- Will Rogers

"Let us have faith that right makes might. And in that faith, let us do our duty to the end, as we understand it."

- President Abraham Lincoln

"You cannot hold a man down without staying down with him."

- Booker T. Washington

"The whole history of the American Revolutionary War is one of false hopes and temporary devices. We must champion more lasting solutions."

- President George Washington

Values, Ideals

Individuals and organizations amass values based upon a series of experiences. Often, values depend upon the context and reflect the facets of professional achievement:

1. Core Industry...The Business You're In.
2. Rendering the Service...Administering Your Work.
3. Accountability...Qualities with Which You Work.
4. Your Relationships Contributions to Other People... Colleagues, Stakeholders.
5. Professional-Leadership Development...Your Path to the Future.
6. Your Contributions to the Organization's Overall

Goals...Your Place in its Big Picture.
7. Body of Work...Your Accomplishments to Date and
   Anticipated Future Output.

Organizations must periodically assess and review their value systems as part of Strategic Planning and corporate Visioning processes. Every business leader should likewise develop and commit to nurturing their own personal value statement.

Here are some examples of Core Values which could be included:

1. To be truthful, forceful and forthright in personal relationships.
2. To treat others as I would like to be treated.
3. To expect that I deserve and will receive the best out of life.
4. To be the kind of person that others can count upon, like, love and admire.
5. To be true to my word and consistent in my actions.
6. To show loyalty and commitment to those causes and projects which I undertake.
7. To show loyalty and commitment to family and those friends who are important to me.
8. To never stop growing emotionally and continuing my journey.

Here are some examples of Strategic Priorities which could be included:

1. To be the best that I can be.
2. To be the best in my chosen field.
3. To create new applications and set new standards for my chosen field.
4. To successfully mentor others.
5. To creatively approach projects in ways that others did not or could not do.
6. To achieve results that are realistically attained and honestly reached.

7. To continue building respect for myself and the self-assuredness to stay focused.
8. To know that I am doing the right things and taking the best possible courses of action.
9. To never stop growing professionally and continuing to evolve to the next tiers.

VISION

"I have a dream."

- Martin Luther King, Jr.

"Pure logic is the ruin of the spirit."

- Antoine de Saint-Exupery

"I've got vision, and the rest of the world is wearing bifocals."
- Paul Newman, "Butch Cassidy and the Sundance Kid"

"The reasonable man adapts himself to the world. The unreasonable man persists in trying to adapt the world to himself. Therefore, all progress depends on the unreasonable man."

- George Bernard Shaw

"We are like dwarves upon the shoulders of giants, and so able to see more and farther than the ancients."

- Bernard of Chartres

"People only see what they are prepared to see."
- Ralph Waldo Emerson

"A moment's insight is worth a life's experience."
- Supreme Court Justice Oliver Wendell Holmes

"A danger foreseen is half avoided."

- Thomas Fuller

"Vision is the art of seeing things invisible."

- Jonathan Swift

"Two men look out through the same bars. One sees the mud, and one the stars."

- Frederick Langbridge

"If I can see so far, it's because I stand on the shoulders of giants."

- Sir Isaac Newton

"The four measures of a person's reason for being are courage, judgment, integrity and dedication."

- President-elect John F. Kennedy

"You've got to have a dream. If you don't have a dream, how are you gonna have your dream come true?"

- Richard Rodgers and Oscar Hammerstein, "South Pacific"

"We go where our vision is."

- Joseph Murphy

"Every moment is a golden one for him who has the vision to recognize it as such."

- Henry Miller

"Every creator painfully experiences the chasm between his inner vision and its ultimate expression."

- Isaac Bashevis Singer

"Where there is no vision, people perish."

- The Bible

"You are not here merely to make a living. You are here to enable the world to live more amply, with greater vision, and with a finer spirit of hope and achievement. You are here to enrich the world. You impoverish yourself if you forget this errand."

- President Woodrow Wilson

"For visions come not to polluted eyes."

- Mary Howitt

Vision

Most organizations know why they exist and their purpose. Those fundamental elements constitute a Mission Statement.

Most organizations never go past the Mission Statement. Thus, they fail to realize potential. Having a purpose by itself does not make the organization materialize, much less be successful.

Visioning is the process where good ideas become something more. Visioning is a catalyst toward long-term evaluation, planning and implementation. Visioning is a jump-off point by which forward-thinking organizations ask: What will we look like in the future? What do we want to become? How will we evolve? Vision is a realistic picture of what is possible.

Businesses, communities and organizations will succeed by having, communicating and garnering support for a Shared Vision. Visioning sets the stage for necessary processes, such as growth strategies, re-engineering, training, enhancing shareholder value and organizational development.

Without visioning, the community simply performs band-aid surgery on problems as they occur. The Vision provides continuous guidance to employees at every level as to how they should manage their respective responsibilities.

Visioning must be Big Picture in perspective. It must creatively focus upon the whole and then the parts of the organization, as they relate to the whole. It is a process by which a Strategic Plan and Visioning program components come off the shelf and alive into action, relative to all levels of the organization:

1. Resource. Equipment, tools, materials, schedules.
2. Skills-Tasks. Duties, activities, tasks, behaviors, attitudes, contracting, project fulfillment.
3. Role-Job. Assignments, responsibilities, functions, relationships, accountability.
4. Systems-Processes. Structure, hiring, control, work design, supervision, decisions.
5. Strategy. Planning, tactics, organizational development.
6. Culture-Mission. Values, customs, beliefs, goals, objectives, benchmarking.
7. Philosophy. Organizational purpose, vision, quality of life, ethics, long-term growth.

The Vision describes what can and will happen, once everyone's energies are focused. Vision is not a financial forecast or a market analysis. Vision is less of a dream and more of a realistic picture of what is possible. When there is a genuine Vision (as compared to a terse "vision statement"), people are compelled to learn and excel...not because they are told to but because they want to.

Most leaders have personal visions that rarely get communicated to the organization. By default, Vision has resolved around the values and positioning of one leader. Often, a crisis will rally the organization, but that tends to be short-lived.

Given the choice, most people and their organizations will pursue high goals. Visioning is a process that melds individual visions into a recipe for success...a shared set of guiding practices. When different constituencies have common visions (or at least applications of them), they will bond together for purpose and cause.

Personal visions are driven by an individual's deep caring. Shared visions derive their power via common caring. Truly, people want to be connected together.

Shared visions take time to emerge. They grow as a result of successful showcasing of individual visions, with benchmarks for success that are understood. Ongoing conversation is required to foster shared visions. Out of listening, insights of what is possible shall emerge.

The key elements of Strategic Vision are:
1. Business scope and scale.
2. Product and market focus.
3. Competitive focus.
4. Orientation toward image and relationships.
5. Applicability to organization and culture.

Visioning needs to take place within each business unit, as well as at the larger organizational level. Too often, management fails to articulate its values or does so imperfectly.

The purposes and expected benefits of Visioning include:
- Taking hold of the future.
- Setting something in motion that will honor those who have built the organization.
- Involving the widest base of support in pro-active change and growth.
- Benchmarking the progress made and communicating it to outside constituencies.
- Nurturing the organization's image.
- Understanding the difference between good and bad handling of crises.
- Crisis follow-ups that help heal and rebuild after problems... versus those that fester and bring destruction to organizations.
- Study and ready the organization to make best advantage of bridge-building and problem remediation concepts.
- Methodologies to address problems sooner, rather than later.
- Establishing safeguards against future trouble.
- Putting more emphasis upon the positive ingredients

and happenings.

WORK

"There is no substitute for hard work."

- Thomas A. Edison

"I don't want to achieve immortality through my work. I want to achieve it through not dying."

- Woody Allen

"Blessed is he who has found his work. Let him ask no other blessedness. Work is the grand cure of all the maladies and miseries that ever beset mankind."

- Thomas Carlyle

"Work is not the curse, but drudgery is."

- Henry Ward Beecher

"More men are killed by overwork than the importance of the world justifies."

- Rudyard Kipling

"The best prize that life offers is the chance to work hard at work worth doing."

- President Theodore Roosevelt

"No bees, no honey. No work, no money."

- Proverb

"Work is much more fun than fun."

- Noel Coward

"When work is a pleasure, life is a joy. When work is a duty, life is slavery."

- Maxim Gorky

"It's been a hard day's night, and I've been working like a dog."
- John Lennon & Paul McCartney

"They say hard work never hurt anybody. But, I figure, why take the chance."
- President Ronald Reagan

"Work is the curse of the drinking classes."
- Oscar Wilde

"Work is necessary for man. Man invented the alarm clock."
- Pablo Piccasso

"Life is too short to do anything for oneself that one can pay others to do for one. It is not wealth one asks for, but just enough to preserve one's dignity, to work unhampered, to be generous, frank and independent."
- W. Somerset Maugham

"If people only knew how hard I work to gain my mastery, it wouldn't seem so wonderful at all."
- Michelangelo Buonarroti

"Temptation rarely comes in working hours. It is in their leisure time that men are made or marred."
- W. N. Taylor

"Working in the garden gives me a profound feeling of inner peace." Ruth Stout "In reality, serendipity accounts for one percent of the blessings we receive in life, work and love. The other 99 percent is due to our efforts."
- Peter McWilliams

"Trouble is only an opportunity in work clothes."
- Henry J. Kaiser

"I don't believe in intuition. When you get sudden flashes of perception, it is just the brain working faster than usual. But you've been getting ready to know it for a long time, and when

it comes, you feel you've known it always."
- Katherine Anne Porter

"The secret of joy in work is contained in one word - excellence. To know how to do something well is to enjoy it."
- Pearl Buck, "The Joy of Children," 1964

"I am doomed to an eternity of compulsive work. No set goal achieved satisfies. Success only breeds a new goal. The golden apple devoured has seeds. It is endless."
- Bette Davis

Work

There is no substitute for good, hard work. These are the seven basic categories of the work force:

1. People who only do the things necessary to get by. Just a series of jobs...no more, no less.
2. People who are managed by others to meet quotas, schedules, procedures and statistics. People who do and make things.
3. Administrative, managerial support. Keep the boat afloat. Push paper, systems, technology. Process is the driving force.
4. System upholders. Don't rock the boat. Maintain the status quo. Resist change. Surround with like minds. Motivated by survival.
5. People who sell something. Most companies have revenue-sales as their primary objective and measurement. To them, everything else is really secondary.
6. People in transition. Forced by circumstances to change (career obsolescence, down-sizing, marketplace factors). Some voluntarily effected changes, to achieve balance or new direction in life. Some do better in newer environments. Others cannot weather changes (too tied to staid corporate

orientations).

7. Idealists...out to do meaningful things. Deeply committed to accomplishing something special... beyond basic job requirements. Adapt to and benefit from change. Learn to take risks. Motivated by factors other than money.

In each category of the work force, those employees subscribe to one of these seven plateaus of work ethic:

1. Just Enough to Get By. Getting paid is the objective. Don't know or have not learned anything further.
2. Taking Advantage of the System. Coffee break mentality. Abuse sick day policies, health benefits, etc. "Never gonna be" syndrome.
3. Inside the Box. Follow the rules but never consider formulating them. Subscribe to the philosophy: "There are no wise decisions...only activities carried out according to company procedures."
4. Don't Rock the Boat. Interested in remaining gainfully employed. Look forward in the short-term to the next paid vacation, in the long-term toward retirement.
5. Professional Is As Professional Does. Daily behaviors, achievements speak for themselves. Consistent in approaches. Never stop learning and growing.
6. Change Agent. Either forced by circumstances to change (career obsolescence, down-sizing, marketplace factors) or thrive upon change. As time progresses, become a mentor and champion for change.
7. Deep Commitments to Body of Work, Professionalism, Ethics. Don't know what a coffee break, sick day or vacation is. Give their lives, souls, expertise to careers and the lifetime results show positively. Profound influence.

YOUTH

"No wise man ever wished to be younger."

- Jonathan Swift

"Youth is something very new. Twenty years ago, no one mentioned it."

- Coco Chanel

"A majority of young people seem to develop arteriosclerosis forty years before they get the physical kind."

- Aldous Huxley

"No young man believes he shall ever die."

- William Hazlitt

"Youth is a malady of which one becomes cured a little every day."

- Benito Mussolini

"The young will always have the same problem...how to rebel and conform at the same time. They have now solved this by defying their parents and copying one another."

- Quentin Crisp

"One starts to get young at the age of 60, and then it is too late."

- Pablo Piccasso

"Far too good to waste on children."

- George Bernard Shaw

"Live as long as you may. The first twenty years are the longest half of your life."

- Robert Southey

"It is an illusion that youth is happy, an illusion of those who have lost it; but the young know they are wretched for they are full of the truthless ideal which have been instilled into them, and each time they come in contact with the real, they are bruised and wounded."

- W. Somerset Maugham

"There's nothing that keeps its youth, so far as I know, but a tree and truth."

- Supreme Court Justice Oliver Wendell Holmes

"Young people are in a condition like permanent intoxication, because youth is sweet and they are growing."

- Aristotle

"There are admirable potentialities in every human being. Believe in your strength and your youth. Learn to repeat endlessly to yourself, 'It all depends on me.'"

- Andre Gide

"I do nothing but go about persuading you all, old and young alike, not to take thought for your persons or your properties, but and chiefly to care about the greatest improvement of the soul. I tell you that virtue is not given by money, but that from virtue comes money and every other good of man, public as well as private. This is my teaching, and if this is the doctrine which corrupts the youth, I am a mischievous person."

- Socrates

"Praise youth and it will prosper."

- Irish Proverb

"Don't laugh at a youth for his affectations. He is only trying on one face after another to find his own."

- Logan Pearsall Smith

"Keep true to the dreams of thy youth."

- Friedrich von Schiller

"Youth cannot know how age thinks and feels. But old men are

guilty if they forget what it was to be young."
- *J. K. Rowling*, "Harry Potter and the Order of the Phoenix"

"There are three things which the superior man guards against. In youth...lust. When he is strong...quarrelsomeness. When he is old...covetousness."

- Confucius

Youth

These are the biggest mistakes made by young people at the beginning of their careers:

1. Desires. Want the status that others have. Their primary career motivation is money and the power it can bring. They want to be paid for everything they do. They don't learn how to be a joiner and, thus, cannot ascend as a leader.
2. Attitude. Many believe that riches and success are due to them instantly, saying they are trying hard when they're not. Some use, abuse and knowingly waste the time of others, notably their supervisors. There are some that always have an excuse.

3. Work Ethic. Some people want a job, not a career. They learn how to cover tracks and justify excuses. Always looking somewhere else, without appreciating the opportunities at hand.

4. Education, Training, Professional Development. For some, there exists an unwillingness to learn. Some seek to be a carbon copy of someone else, thus the failure to pursue professional development. Some people think their academic credentials make them superior to persons in other professions. Many are clueless as to what business ethics or quality management principles are all about...which come with executive seasoning.

5. People Skills. There is a failure to develop people skills, due to a lack of upbringing about the subtleties and contexts inherent in

business life. Failure to show proper respect toward elders tends to stunt leadership development. For some, it's always someone else's fault, due to an inability to identify their own shortcomings or limitations.

6. Organizational Savvy. The failure to pay sufficient dues leads to misplaced ambitions and careers. Many wrongfully assume they are a senior member of the profession when they never mastered being an effective junior, let alone mastering the middle career years. It is essential to learn proactive attitude, positive marketplace grammar, etiquette, business savvy and common courtesies in order to be an effective leader.

7. Body of Work. Those who will not go the distance or see their careers as a long-term set of challenges will not succeed, thus bringing their companies down. Some maintain the "I can do that" mentality...challenging seasoned professionals. The failure to understand either the Big Picture or the small pieces needed to implement it leads to a myopic and partial view of business.

Here are some characteristics of young people (rising stars) will make it as professionals and business leaders:

- Act as though they will one day be management.
- Think as a manager, not as a worker.
- Learn and do the things it will take to assume management responsibility.
- Be mentored by others.
- Act as a mentor to still others.
- Don't expect status overnight.
- Measure their output and expect to be measured as a profit center to the company.
- Learn to pace...and be in the chosen career for the long-run.
- Don't expect someone else to be the rescuer or cut corners in the path to artificial success.
- Learn from failures, reframing them as opportunities.
- Learn to expect, predict, understand and relish

success.
- Behave as a gracious winner.
- Acquire visionary perception.
- Study and utilize marketing and business development
  techniques.
- Contribute to the bottom line...directly and indirectly.
- Offer value-added service.
- Never stop paying dues...and   see this continuum as
  "continuous quality improvement."
- Study and comprehend the subtleties of life.
- Never stop learning, growing and doing. In short,
  never stop!

CLOSING QUOTES

"Go for the gusto. Live life, every golden minute of it."
- Schlitz Beer commercial

"If I can dream of a better land, where all my brothers live hand in hand, tell me why my dreams can't come true."
- Elvis Presley/Mac Davis

"When you move real slow, it seems like mo', 'cause it's alright."
- Curtis Mayfield

"Move on up...to your destination."
- Curtis Mayfield

"If I can begin to teach you...how to give a damn about your fellow man."
- Spanky and Our Gang

"The games people play now. Every night and every day now. Never meaning what they say. Never saying what they mean."
- Joe South

"Come on, baby, let's start today. Come on, baby, let's play the Game of Love."
- Wayne Fontana and the Mindbenders

"When too halves are gone, there's nothing left. Nothing from nothing doesn't give you much to work with."
- Foghorn Leghorn, "Looney Toons"

"Changes in attitudes, changes in latitudes."
- Jimmy Buffett

About the author...
Hank Moore Futurist, Corporate Strategist™

Hank Moore is an internationally known organizational-business advisor, speaker and author. He is a Big Picture strategist, with original, cutting-edge ideas for creating, implementing and sustaining corporate growth throughout every sector of the organization. He is a Futurist and Corporate Strategist™, with four trademarked concepts of business...heralded widely for ways to remediate corporate damage, enhance productivity and facilitate better business.

Moore is among the highest level of business overview expert and is in the rarified circle of experts including Peter Drucker, Tom Peters, Steven Covey, Peter Senge and W. Edwards Deming. Drucker termed Hank Moore's Business Tree™ as the most original business model of the past 40 years.

As a Futurist and Corporate Strategist™, Hank Moore advises organizations about growth strategies, visioning, planning, executive-leadership development, futurism and the Big Picture issues which profoundly affect their future.

His Business Tree™ is a trademarked approach to growing, strengthening and evolving business, while mastering change, with the result being the companies' destinies being charted.

Moore has provided senior level advising services for more than 5,000 client organizations (including 100 of the Fortune 500), public sector entities, companies in transition (startup, re- engineering, mergers, going public),professional associations and non-profit organizations. He has worked with all major industries over a 40-year career. He advises at the Executive Committee and board levels, providing Big Picture ideas.

Moore assists business specialists on enlarging their scope and taking up mantles of greater responsibility and recognition. Moore has overseen 400 strategic plans and corporate visioning processes. He has conducted 300+ assessments of organizations.

He has won more than 150 awards for client work and community stewardship.

Benefits of Moore's Big Picture consultancy include:

▪ Understanding how and why The Business Tree™ (any organization) stands and grows, instead of looking at each leaf, twig or branch.

▪ Inspiring executives to think holistically about each component of the business in terms of the Big Picture, master change and take companies to new tiers.

▪ Fresh approaches toward reapplying past knowledge and experiences. These become Lessons Learned But Not Soon Forgotten.

▪ Strategies to reduce The High Cost of Doing Nothing... making business more creative, effective and profitable.

Client Advising-Consulting Activities

▪ Company reorganizations
▪ Taking clients public
▪ Strategic Planning
▪ Marketplace repositioning
▪ Community stewardship
▪ Corporate Visioning
▪ Crisis management-preparedness
▪ Growth Strategies programs
▪ Quality management
▪ Reorganizing board of directors
▪ Creative idea generation
▪ Re-engineering
▪ Mergers & Acquisitions
▪ Executive Think Tanks Performance reviews
▪ Non-profit consultation

- Board & CEO advising
- Big Picture viewpoint

Categories of Speaking Engagements

- Executive Think Tanks for corporate leadership.
- Association and corporate leadership development institutes.
- Economic development symposia and conference Futurism keynoter.
- Instructing business leaders how to conduct Strategic Planning.

Books by Hank Moore

- The Business Tree™: Growth Strategies and Tactics for Surviving and Thriving
- The High Cost of Doing Nothing: Why Good Companies Go Bad
- The Classic Television Reference: A Mirror of Societal Changes
- The $50,000 Business Makeover Marathon
- The Future Has Moved...and Left No Forwarding Address
- Power Stars to Light the Flame... The Visionaries and You

On the Web:
http://www.hankmoore.com
You Tube:
http://www.youtube.com/watch?v=wZ8h18hMsCo
Facebook:
http://www.facebook.com/hank.moore.10
LinkedIn
http://www.linkedin.com/profile/view?
id=43004647&trk=tabpro